THEATRE ROYAL
— STRATFORD EAST —

10 June – 9 July
Theatre Royal Stratford East presents the world premiere of

TAKEAWAY

Book and Lyrics by Robert Lee

Music by Leon Ko

First performed at Theatre Royal Stratford East
on Friday 10 June 2011

Book and Lyrics by **Robert Lee**
Music by **Leon Ko**

Cast (in alphabetical order):

Reese **Marcus Ellard**
Eddie **Stephen Hoo**
Dillon **Natasha Jayetileke**
Widow Chu **Pik-sen Lim**
Lum **Windson Liong**
Sheila **Gloria Onitiri**
Guardian Angel **Shelley Williams**
Angela **Gabby Wong**
Henry **Ozzie Yue**
Band **Simona Budd**
      Stanley Long
      Isabella Pek
      Mimi Ueoka

Creative team

Book and Lyrics **Robert Lee**
Music **Leon Ko**
Director **Kerry Michael**
Set & Costume Designer **Foxton**
Musical Director **Robert Hyman**
Choreographer **Jason Pennycooke**
Lighting Designer **Paul Anderson**
Sound Designer **John Leonard**
Associate Choreographer **Farrah Hussain**
Assistant Director **Amy Ip**
Casting **Sookie McShane CDG** and **Lucy Jenkins CDG**

Production credits

Production Manager **Simon Sturgess**
Deputy Stage Manager **CJ Mitchell**
Assistant Stage Manager **Kerry Sullivan**
Costume Supervisor **Alison Cartledge**
Dresser **Emma Seychell**
Assistant Electrician **Alice Afflick-Mensah**
Follow spot operators **Anne Scholze** and **David Train**
Flyman **Dave Munday**
Video Realisation: **Chris Lincé**
Scenic Artist: **Magnus Irvine**
Scenic elements built by **Object Construction**
        and **Theatre Royal Stratford East Workshop**
Lighting hires: **Sparks Theatrical Hire**
Sound hires: **Pressure Wave Audio**

Special thanks to

National Theatre Music Department, Intermec,
Royal Mail, Casio, David Mishra, The Octagon Theatre Bolton,
Oldham Coliseum Theatre, New Wolsey Theatre Ipswich,
Colchester Mercury Theatre, bell percussion (www.bellperc.com),
Chris Shum

Cast (in alphabetical order):

Marcus Ellard Reese

Marcus trained at Drama Centre London. Theatre Royal Stratford East credits include: Ben the Woodcutter in RED RIDING HOOD; Colin in MARTINA COLE'S TWO WOMEN, Tosher in COME DANCING – winner of the Whatsonstage.com Award for Best Off-West End Musical; Don Dini in the Olivier-nominated CINDERELLA. Theatre credits include: Ray the Blade in Les Enfants Terribles' THE VAUDEVILLAINS (Latitude Festival and Pleasance Edinburgh); Reuben Smart in THE DIARY OF A CHAV (Workshop Production at Tristan Bates Theatre); Frank Bishop in FAILED STATES (Pleasance Edinburgh) and Alfie in MY DAYS (Drama Centre at Soho Theatre). For more information see www.sainou.com

Stephen Hoo Eddie Woo

Theatre credits include: SOHO STREETS (Soho Theatre); BODEGA LUNG FAT (Hackney Empire Studio); WAKE (National Reisopera Holland); KICK OFF (Riverside Studios); FIT (Drill Hall). Television credits include: EXCLUDED (BBC) and DAY OF THE KAMIKAZE (Channel 4). Film credits include: FIT and KICKOFF. Stephen Hoo was born and raised in London and studied Theatre at The Brit School. He then went on to study Modern and Classical Chinese at The School of Oriental and African Studies (University of London), where he also studied Film & Theatre of China, Taiwan and the Diaspora. Recently he was a guest speaker for Channel 4's Diversity Week and Inspiration Day. Stephen is also a budding playwright and film-maker and a close collaborator with Writer & Director Rikki Beadle-Blair. For more information visit www.stephenhoo.com

Natasha Jayetileke Dillon

Natasha trained at Laine Theatre Arts prior to gaining a MA (Cantab) degree from Cambridge University. West End theatre credits include: Sarabi (understudy Nala) in THE LION KING (Lyceum); UK and Greece in EUROBEAT (Novello and National Tour); Handmaiden and Apache soloist in JOSEPH AND THE AMAZING TECHNICOLOR DREAMCOAT (New London) and she created the role of Draupadi for Nitin Sawhney and Stephen Clarke's world premiere of

MAHABHARATA (Sadler's Wells and National Tour).
Other theatre credits include: Victoria in NOVERO (Germany);
Princess Jasmine in ALADDIN (Civic Theatre Chelmsford
and Camberley Theatre); Tiger Lily in PETER PAN (Theatre
Royal, Plymouth, Churchill Theatre, Bromley, Mayflower Theatre,
Southampton and New Theatre, Cardiff) and THAT'S THE
WAY I LIKE IT (Epsom Playhouse). Television credits include:
ULTIMATE MOVIE TOONS (ITV), HUSTLE (BBC),
ALADDIN (LWT), THIS MORNING (ITV), THE VANESSA
SHOW (BBC), NICK NEWS (Nickleodeon) and The Mag
(Channel 5). Film credits include: BEYOND BOUNDARIES and
THE MISTRESS OF SPICES. Natasha's radio appearances range
from BBC 5 Live and BBC 3 to Radio Tokyo. She also features on
the soundtrack of the feature film PRIDE (Lionsgate) composed by
Aaron Zigman.

 Pik-sen Lim Widow Chu
Theatre credits include: MOON WALKING
IN CHINA TOWN (Soho Theatre); THREE
THOUSAND THREADS (Stella Quines Theatre
Co); FESTIVAL FOR THE FISH (Yellow Earth);
ROMEO & JULIET (Haymarket; Basingstoke);
TAKEAWAY (Mu-Lan Productions); and
CHINOISERIE (Royal Court Theatre). Television work includes
RUBY IN THE SMOKE (BBC); SPIRIT WARRIORS (CBBC);
THE BILL (Fremantle/Thames); DON'T STOP DREAMING
(Media; What Else?); LITTLE BRITAIN (BBC); PATRICK'S
PLANET (Tiger Lily/ CBBC); FORTY SOMETHING (Carlton
TV); NIGHT AND DAY (LWT); LONDON'S BURNING
(LWT); CASUALTY (BBC); MEDICS (Granada) and DR
WHO (BBC). Pik-sen has just finished filming the role of Killer
Cleaner in the sequel feature film JOHNNY ENGLISH REBORN
with Rowan Atkinson due for release Autumn 2011. Other film
credits include GRANNY'S GHOST (Kalmboy Films); DON'T
STOP DREAMING (What Else? Ltd); PLENTY (Dir: Fred
Schepisi). Other credits MIRANDA (Dir: Marc Munden); THE
MONKEY KING (Hallmark Films); ARABIAN NIGHTS
(Henson Productions) and FIERCE CREATURES (Dir: Fred
Schepisi). Radio work includes THE FURTHER ADVENTURES
OF SHERLOCK HOLMES; SCUMDOG MILLIONAIRE;
CHAIRMAN MAO - THE UNTOLD STORY; ORCHID
CHERRY BLOSSOM; SKY BURIAL; WORDS ON A NIGHT
BREEZE; WILD SWANS; THE JOY LUCK CLUB (all for BBC
Radio 4) and MADE IN CHINA (BBC World Service).

Windson Liong Lum
Training: Central School of Speech and Drama. Theatre credits in UK include: INTO THE WOODS and HAGRIDDEN (Embassy Theatre). OUTSIDE UK: IF THERE ARE SEASONS and ARMY DAZE (Drama Centre); I AM QUEEN (Drama Centre Black Box); FIVE FOOT BROADWAY and MOONBIRD (Esplanade Studio Theatre); SHANGHAI BLUES (Esplanade Theatre); ROSES AND HELLO (The Arts House); IMMORTALX (Jubilee Hall); SUMMER SWARM OF SONGS, YOU ARE SPECIAL (AGF Theatre); THE WIZ (DBS Arts Centre). Television credits include: DADDY'S GIRLS, INCREDIBLE TALES, TRUE COURAGE and @MOULMEIN HIGH (MediaCorp Studios, Singapore). Film credits include: AFTER SCHOOL (Gateway Entertainment).

Gloria Onitiri Sheila
Gloria studied English and Drama at the University of Birmingham and spent two years as a member of the National Youth Music Theatre playing Morgan Le Fay in PENDRAGON (Northcott Theatre, Minack theatre, Peacock Theatre, Edinburgh Festival Theatre and Japan) and originated the role of Sylvia in THE DREAMING (Northcott Theatre and Lindbury Studio, Royal Opera House). Recent work includes: Arion in Cressida Brown's AMPHIBIANS (Bridewell Theatre); a successful 2 year engagement as Nala in Disney's THE LION KING at the Lyceum Theatre and she features as Knightriss in the new children's gameshow series, SPLATALOT, for the BBC, YTV Canada and ABC Australia (premieres here in June). Other theatre work: Simone in BEEN SO LONG (Rehearsed reading, Young Vic); Aisha, Juliettte and Violca in HURRIED STEPS (New Shoes Theatre); Understudy Mrs Thistletwat/ Girl Bear, Kate/Lucy and Gary Coleman in AVENUE Q (Original Cast, Noel Coward Theatre); Bachaae in THE BACHAAE (National Theatre of Scotland); Miss Sherman in FAME (Tour Holland). Television: Dotun in THE WINDOW (IWC Media, C4); Marcia in BAD GIRLS (Shed Productions); Donna in GRASS (BBC Comedy). Film: Jackie in RESURRECTING THE STREET WALKER (Scala Films).

Shelley Williams Guardian Angel
Theatre credits include: UP AGAINST THE
WALL (Bolton Octagon Theatre); ANNOWON'S
SONG (Tricycle Theatre); JACK AND THE
BEANSTALK (Barbican); DADDY COOL The
Musical (Shaftesbury Theatre); HAIR (The Octagon
Theatre); I TREASURE OUR SECRET (The
King's Head); SUPPOSED TO LIVE (Pleasance Theatre); BLUE
GIRL (Vienna's English Theatre); SWEET SOUL MUSIC (The
Solvedore); SLEEPING BEAUTY (The Paul Robeson Theatre);
POISON (Tricycle Theatre); ROMEO AND JULIET (Open Air
Theatre); TWILIGHT (Voices in the Dark Theatre Company – Tour);
ALADDIN (The North Cheshire Lodge); SEPTIMUS SEVERUS
(Collective Artistes). Film includes: BALLAST (Manchester Film
festival); TWO MINDS (Off the Cuff Productions). Shelley has also
performed on Radio and as a vocalist has performed and recorded
with a number of music artistes some of which include M people and
Westlife. Shelley would like to thank Gloria Griffiths for being her
Welsh inspiration.

Gabby Wong Angela
Originally from Hong Kong, Gabby is fluent in
English and Cantonese, as well as being conversational
in Mandarin and German. Whilst studying Politics
at University of Bath, she became heavily involved in
the student theatre which saw her perform at NSDF
and Edinburgh Festival. She then went on to train
professionally on the Acting course at Italia Conti and has worked on
varying ventures since graduation. Gabby is a founding member and
resident writer/ producer for independent film company GRfilms.
Credits include: OTHELLO (Shakespeare's Globe); GIANT &
HERO (Birmingham Rep); STOCKHOLM (3P Entertainment);
CLOUD NINE (Pleasance, Edinburgh); DIALOGUE &
REBUTTAL and DREAM OF RED PAVILIONS (Yellow Earth);
INTO THE WOODS (Landor Theatre); AVENUE OF ETERNAL
PEACE (BBC Radio 4) and RANDOM 11 (Vertigo Heights).

Ozzie Yue Henry

Theatre credits include: CIGGIE RUN (St Helen's Theatre Royal); ONE STEP FORWARD ONE STEP BACK (for Liverpool Capital Culture, Dreamthinkspeak); MOONWALKING IN CHINA TOWN (Soho Theatre); KENSUKE'S KINGDOM (Birmingham, London, Dubai, UK Tour); 3000 TROUBLED THREADS (Edinburgh Lyceum); HAMLET (Singapore Repertory Theatre). Television includes: RAB C NESBIT (Comedy Unit); COME FLY WITH ME (BBC); WHITE VAN MAN (BBC); KATY BRAND'S BIG ASS SHOW (World's End TV); THE ADAM AND SHELLEY SHOW (Granada); ULTIMATE FORCE IV (Bentley); ROCKET MAN (BBC); CASUALTY (BBC); SILENT WITNESS (BBC); WILLIAM AND MARY(Granada); EUSTACE BROTHERS (BBC); NCS-MANHUNT, (BBC); FATHER TED (Hat Trick Productions); HARRY (BBC); ALL QUIET ON THE PRESTON FRONT / PRESTON FRONT (BBC). Film includes: RAFTA RAFTA (Left Bank Pictures); ACT OF GRACE (Embrace Pictures); CHARLIE NOADES RIP (North Star Productions); BEZAUBERNDE NANNY (Studio Hamburg); SYRIANA (Warner Brothers); CHROMOPHOBIA (Chromo (IOM) Ltd); THE LOST FLEET OF KHUBLAI KHAN (Atlantic Productions); OUT FOR THE KILL (Millennium Films); LARA CROFT-TOMB RAIDER, (Paramount British Pictures); CROUPIER (Little Bird). For more information see www.sainou.com

Creative team

Robert Lee Bookwriter/lyricist
Robert is a lyricist and librettist whose original musicals include
JOURNEY TO THE WEST (music by Leon Ko), HEADING
EAST (music by Ko) and THE SWEET BY AND BY (book and
music by Maria V.S. Seigenthaler). His work as a music director
includes the recordings STAGE 1 and STAGE 2 and the premiere
cast recording of HEADING EAST (DINK Records). He and
Ko received the 2001 Richard Rodgers Development Award for
HEADING EAST and an AT&T First Stage Grant for the musical
CHINESE HELL, developed with producer Margo Lion and San
Francisco's American Conservatory Theater. Recently, he and Ko were
commissioned by East of Doheny to create a musical stage adaptation
of Jean Kerr's PLEASE DON'T EAT THE DAISIES. Robert is an
alumnus of Princeton University and the Graduate Musical Theatre
Writing Program at NYU's Tisch School of the Arts (where he
currently serves on the faculty) and is an Artistic Associate at Theatre
Royal Stratford East in London, where he leads its Musical Theatre
Writing Workshop with composer Fred Carl. The Workshop is the
subject of the film RAPPIN' AT THE ROYAL (Blast Films, 2005).
He is a member of the Dramatists Guild.

Leon Ko Composer
Leon received his Master's degree in Musical Theatre Writing
from New York University's Tisch School of the Arts. His
musical HEADING EAST (with book and lyrics by Robert Lee)
won the 2001 Richard Rodgers Development Award. His works were
performed at Carnegie Hall and on Public Broadcasting Service in the
US. Ko won Best Score for his four Cantonese musicals at the Hong
Kong Theatre Awards. For his work on the film PERHAPS
LOVE (2005), he received a Golden Horse Award in Taiwan, a Hong
Kong Film Award, an Asia-Pacific Film Festival Award and a Golden
Bauhinia Award. He was nominated for Best Original Score again
in 2008 for his contributions to the movie THE WARLORDS. Ko
was the musical director of Hong Kong pop legend Jacky Cheung's
2004 world tour of SNOW, WOLF, LAKE. In 2006 he wrote a
new music for the classic Cantonese opera PRINCESS CHANG-
PING. In 2010, he wrote music for the play THE LIAISONS for
the Hong Kong Arts Festival and Fredric Mao Theatre Project,
which was presented at the Expo 2010 Shanghai. Besides music,
he launched TIME IN A BOTTLE, the first-ever perfume bottle
exhibition in Hong Kong in 2010, showcasing the artistry of vintage
bottles in the context of theatre.

Kerry Michael Director

Kerry was appointed the Artistic Director and Chief Executive of Theatre Royal Stratford East in September 2004. Since then he has upheld the Theatre's commitment to develop new work and to provide a platform for those voices under-represented in the ever-changing communities of East London. In 2007 Theatre Royal was nominated for an Olivier Award for 'presenting a powerful season of provocative work that reaches new audiences'. Its hip-hop dance production PIED PIPER won an Olivier the same year. The following year, Kerry's production of CINDERELLA was nominated for an Olivier, the first pantomime nominated in the Awards' history. Kerry's most recent directing credits include I WAS LOOKING AT THE CEILING AND THEN I SAW THE SKY, a co-production with Barbican; THE GREAT EXTENSION in 2009; THE HARDER THEY COME, which obtained wide critical acclaim transferring to the Barbican and the Playhouse Theatre in the West End before going on a very successful tour of Canada and the US; and Ray Davies' COME DANCING. Kerry is the chair of Stratford Rising; a trustee of Discover, which provides creative, play and learning opportunities for children and their carers in Stratford; and a member of Equity's International Committee for Artists' Freedom.

Foxton Set & Costume Designer

TAKEAWAY is Foxton's first design for Theatre Royal Stratford East. Design work elsewhere includes: OFFICE SUITE (Theatre Royal Bath & national tour); BRASSED OFF (Sheffield Theatres, national tour), BLUE/ORANGE, THE COUNTRY WIFE & QUEEN'S ENGLISH (Palace Theatre, Watford); A PASSIONATE WOMAN, UP ON THE ROOF, VINCENT IN BRIXTON, THE PRICE & DOUBLE INDEMNITY (New Wolsey Theatre, Ipswich); MARTHA, JOSIE AND THE CHINESE ELVIS, RETURN TO THE FORBIDDEN PLANET, KES, THE SUNSHINE BOYS, PERFECT PITCH, ON THE PISTE & GOOD GOLLY MISS MOLLY(Coliseum Theatre, Oldham); EQUUS, MACBETH, THE MISER & DEAD FUNNY (Salisbury Playhouse); THE RISE & FALL OF LITTLE VOICE (Harrogate Theatre); KVETCH (West Yorkshire Playhouse); ALL MY SONS, NEVILLE'S ISLAND & BRASSED OFF (York Theatre Royal); THINGS WE DO FOR LOVE & DEATH OF A SALESMAN (Library Theatre, Manchester); DESPERATE TO BE DORIS, HECTOR'S HOUSE & THE IMPORTANCE OF BEING EARNEST (LipService national tours); LOOT, PUB QUIZ IS LIFE, MACBETH, THE FLAGS, LADIES DAY, WUTHERING HEIGHTS, 1984, TOAST, UP ON ROOF & UNDER THE

WHALEBACK(Hull Truck); EIGHT MILES HIGH (Royal Court Theatre, Liverpool) and over fifty productions for the Bolton Octagon including AND DID THOSE FEET…, THE CRUCIBLE, THE CARETAKER, FOUR NIGHTS IN KNARESBOROUGH, SAVED, BLOOD WEDDING, A MIDSUMMER NIGHT'S DREAM, DANCING AT LUGHNASA & THE PITCHFORK DISNEY. He has twice been nominated for the TMA design award & has won the Manchester Evening News design award five times, most recently in 2008 for OH WHAT A LOVELY WAR (Octagon Theatre).His work was included in the British exhibit at the Prague Quadrennial (1995), he was a judge of the Linbury Prize (1997). Forthcoming work includes THE WINTER'S TALE (Mercury Theatre, Colchester)

Robert Hyman Musical Director
Robert has worked extensively at Theatre Royal Stratford East for the last 12 years both as a composer and Musical Director. That body of work includes music and lyrics for CINDERELLA (Olivier-nominated), PINOCCHIO, ALADDIN and RED RIDING HOOD (with Trish Cooke); RED RIDING HOOD and DICK WHITTINGTON (with Patrick Prior), as well as songs for the THE SNOW QUEEN and HANSEL AND GRETEL, and scores for 20, 000 LEAGUES UNDER THE SEA and MAKE SOME NOISE. Also Musical Director for the hit musicals THE BIG LIFE (both at Theatre Royal and the West End), Ray Davies' COME DANCING and Stratford East pantos since 1998. Other recent projects include conducting a choir of 5000 at the 02 in LICENSE TO THRILL; Musical Director for the inaugural performance of the World Children's Ensemble at the Royal Albert Hall involving 1500 young people from 37 different countries; Musical Director for the recent hit Graeae tour of REASONS TO BE CHEERFUL and songs/lyrics for Image Musical Theatre Co. whose shows THE SELFISH GIANT, TOM'S MIDNIGHT GARDEN and STIG OF THE DUMP are currently touring the UK. He also works extensively in the training of young people as Musical Director of Theatretrain.

Jason Pennycooke Choreographer
Jason has been working in the performing arts industry for the past 18 years in various capacities. West End theatre includes: CATS (national tour), LA CAGE AUX FOLLES, STARLIGHT EXPRESS, FIVE GUYS NAMED MOE, RENT, THE BIG LIFE, HEY MR. PRODUCER, STOMP, THE RAT PACK, ROBIN AND THE SEEN HOODS and SOUL TRAIN. Other theatre includes: SIMPLY HEAVENLY (Young Vic), GOLDEN BOY (Greenwich

Theatre), and ELEGIES FOR ANGELS, PUNKS AND RAGING QUEENS (The Globe), SAMMY (Theatre Royal Stratford East), TIME FLOWS (Trinity Buoy Wharf) and FOREVER YOUNG (Nottingham Playhouse). Dance credits include: MEL B, THE SPICE GIRLS, MORCHEEBA, TONI BRAXTON, ETERNAL, MICHAEL JACKSON AND MUSE. Advert credits include: COCA-COLA, HALIFAX, CHUPA CHUPS, FORD KA AND FOX KIDS. Film includes: MISTER LONELY (O'Salvation) and SHOPPING (Impact Pictures).

Choreography credits include: the forthcoming CRAZY FOR YOU (Varmlandsoperan Karlstad Sweden), END OF THE RAINBOW (Trafalgar Studios), FIVE GUYS NAMED MOE (Theatre at the Mill, Belfast), HELP THE HEROES (St. George's Day charity match at Twickenham Stadium), I WAS LOOKING AT THE CEILING AND THEN I SAW THE SKY (Theatre Royal Stratford East), HALF A SIXPENCE (national tour), THE BIG LIFE (West End), PORGY AND BESS (West End), PEARL FISHERS (Dorset Opera Company), LET THERE BE LOVE (Tricycle Theatre), SONGS OF FREEDOM (Southbank Centre), THROUGH THE DOOR (Trafalgar Studios), MILLENNIUM MAGIC (Cardiff Millennium Stadium), SAMMY (Theatre Royal Stratford East), TIME FLOWS (Trinity Buoy Wharf), M. J. DAY (Hippodrome/Hammersmith Apollo), UK GARAGE AWARDS, FAME ACADEMY, COMPLETING THE BAND, I WANT YOU BACK by Mel B, and TELL ME by Mel B. With Heather Smalls of M-People, he also set a Guinness World Record with 800 dancers performing for the Help for Heroes London Wasps V Bath Rugby charity match at Twickenham Stadium with Heather Smalls of M-People. He has also received Olivier Award and What's On Stage Award nominations. Jason has also worked on fashion shows for Vidal Sassoon.

Paul Anderson Lighting Designer
Previous productions for Theatre Royal Stratford East include: 20,000 LEAGUES UNDER THE SEA, SHOOT TO WIN, PINNOCHIO, SLEEPING BEAUTY, RED RIDING HOOD, ALADDIN and CINDERELLA. Other theatre includes: EDUCATING RITA and SHIRLEY VALENTINE (also Menier Chocolate Factory), ENDGAME, ARCADIA, TREASURE ISLAND, SWIMMING WITH SHARKS, LITTLE SHOP OF HORRORS, UNDERNEATH THE LINTEL, THE TEMPEST, BENT, ON THE THIRD DAY, SOMEONE WHO'LL WATCH OVER ME, SIMPLY HEAVENLY (also Young Vic), LENNY HENRY'S SO MUCH THINGS TO SAY (also international tour) and A SERVANT TO TWO MASTERS

(all in the West End); BLOOD AND GIFTS, NATION, THE REVENGERS TRAGEDY, A MINUTE TOO LATE, STUFF HAPPENS, A FUNNY THING HAPPENED ON THE WAY TO THE FORUM, MEASURE FOR MEASURE, CYRANO DE BERGERAC AND THE BIRDS (all for the National Theatre); ALL MY SONS (with Katie Holmes, Broadway); THE RESISTIBLE RISE OF ARTURO UI (with Al Pacino, New York); TALENT (Menier Chocolate Factory); JULIUS CAESAR, THE TEMPEST and A SERVANT TO TWO MASTERS (all Royal Shakespeare Company); TWELFTH NIGHT (Shakespeare's Globe at Middle Temple Hall); SINGER, AMERICANS, THE INLAND SEA (Oxford Stage Company); TWO CITIES, PLAYING FOR TIME, TAMING OF THE SHREW (Salisbury Playhouse); SHUN-KIN, A DISAPPEARING NUMBER, STRANGE POETRY (with the LA Philharmonic), THE ELEPHANT VANISHES, LIGHT, MNEMONIC (Drama Desk and Lucille Lortell award), THE CHAIRS (Tony, Drama Desk and Olivier nominations) and THE NOISE OF TIME (all Theatre de Complicite); THE ENCHANTED PIG, KNIGHT OF THE BURNING PESTLE, SIMPLY HEAVENLY, ARABIAN NIGHTS, AS I LAY DYING, TWELFTH NIGHT, GUYS AND DOLLS AND WEST SIDE STORY (Young Vic Theatre); SOME GIRLS ARE BIGGER THAN OTHERS, PINOCCHIO, THE THREESOME AND LYRIC NIGHTS (Lyric Hammersmith); ON TOUR, RANDOM AND INCOMPLETE ACTS OF KINDNESS (Royal Court) and TURN OF THE SCREW (Bristol Old Vic). Opera includes: A DOG'S HEART (ENO).

John Leonard Sound Designer
John Leonard started work in theatre sound almost 40 years ago, during which time he has provided soundtracks for theatres all over the world. He has written an acclaimed guide to theatre sound and is the recipient of Drama Desk and LDI Sound Designer Of The Year awards and Honorary Fellowships from The Guildhall School of Music & Drama and The Hong Kong Academy of Performing Arts. Recent sound designs include: ECSTASY (Hampstead Theatre & West-End); ROCKET TO THE MOON (National Theatre); THE CRIPPLE OF INISHMAAN (Druid Theatre US Tour); AS YOU LIKE IT (Rose Theatre, Kingston); THE MASTER BUILDER, BECKY SHAW (Almeida Theatre); TRIBES (Royal Court Theatre); THE MASTER BUILDER (Chichester); THE SILVER TASSIE (Druid Theatre - Galway & Tour); I WAS LOOKING AT THE CEILING AND THEN I SAW THE SKY (Theatre Royal, Stratford East/Barbican); TRUE WEST (Sheffield Crucible); LONDON ASSURANCE, THE POWER OF YES, ENGLAND

PEOPLE VERY NICE, MUCH ADO ABOUT NOTHING, THE ENCHANTMENT (National Theatre); MEASURE FOR MEASURE, ROPE, WASTE, DUET FOR ONE, THE HOMECOMING (Almeida Theatre); THE GIGLI CONCERT, THE CRIPPLE OF INISHMAAN, LONG DAY'S JOURNEY INTO NIGHT (Druid Theatre – Galway, Dublin, New York and tours); YES, PRIME MINISTER, CYRANO DE BERGERAC, CALENDAR GIRLS, THE CHERRY ORCHARD, TAKING SIDES, COLLABORATIONS (Chichester Festival Theatre); RESTORATION, A MONTH IN THE COUNTRY, PEOPLE AT SEA (Salisbury Playhouse); THE GLASS MENAGERIE (The Gate Theatre Dublin) ; CARRIE'S WAR, DUET FOR ONE, IN CELEBRATION, KEAN, DONKEY'S YEARS, SUMMER AND SMOKE, GLENGARRY GLEN ROSS (West End); TRANSLATIONS (Princeton/Broadway); LEAVES, EMPRESS OF INDIA, THE DRUID SYNGE (Druid Theatre Galway Dublin/Edinburgh/Minneapolis/New York).

Farrah Hussain Associate Choreographer
Farrah graduated in July 2010 from SLP College in Leeds. Upon graduating Farrah toured with FAME the Musical in which she was featured in the ensemble and understudied Iris. She has also performed in a number of corporate gigs and shows. Farrah is delighted to have been given the chance to try her hand at choreography on this production and would like to thank Jason Pennycooke for giving her the opportunity.

Amy Ip Assistant Director
Amy's previous writing and directing credits include two original British Chinese musicals; WHEN YELLOW RIVER MEETS THE THAMES (The Steiner Theatre) and CHANGING FORTUNES (Arts Depot). Amy is also an actress and her credits include: Theatre: AROUND THE WORLD IN EIGHTY DAYS (BAC); five seasons at The Scoop, More London where she was one of the founding company members, her many roles there include: Chorus in AGAMEMNON, Moon Priestess in CHILDREN OF HERCULES, Cheng I Sao in TREASURE ISLAND, King Jaspar in THE LONDON NATIVITY, Puck in A MIDSUMMER'S NIGHT DREAM (UKTT Middle East Tour); SUPERPLAYS RETURN (Soho Theatre) and Ling in the award-winning musical THE EMPEROR'S QUEST (C Venues). Television includes : Sun in CASUALTY. Film includes: Mrs Wang in THE VAMPIRES OF BLOODY ISLAND.

THEATRE ROYAL
STRATFORD EAST

Artistic Director **Kerry Michael**
Executive Director **Mary Caws**

Artistic
Associate Artists **Fred Carl, Robert Lee, Ryan Romain, Ultz, Matthew Xia**
Associate Producer **Karen Fisher**
Assistant to Artistic Director **Rita Mishra**

Administration and Operations
General Manager **Ali Fellows**
Building and Facilities Manager **Graeme Bright**
Operations Coordinator **Velma Fontaine**
Resources/Technical Manager **Stuart Saunders**
Building Maintenance Technician **Steven Nickells**

Archives
Theatre Archivist **Murray Melvin**
Assistant Archivist **Mary Ling**

Finance
Head of Finance **Paul Canova**
Finance Officers **Elinor Jones, Titilayo Onanuga**

Development
Development Coordinator **Emma Louise Norton**

Young People's Work
Head of Young People's Work **Jan Sharkey-Dodds**
Project Manager **Serena B. Robins**
Project Manager **Karlos Coleman**
Assistant Producer **Shawab Iqbal**
'State of the Nation' apprentice **Rameeka Parvez**

Open Stage
Head of Open Stage **Charlotte Handel**
Open Stage Intern **Debo Amon**
Open Stage Volunteers **Sue Ah-Chung, Helal Ahmed, Syriah Bailey, Carrie Beeson, Florence Buckeridge, Monique Campbell, Johannes Douglas, Edem Eyomba, Shawab Iqbal, Shereen Jackman, Tom Johnson, Marcella Kaikai, Gillian Lawrence, Ronny Lavie, Soloman Makaddar, Cathy Maurice-Jones, Helena Morais, Onyejelam Oparaku, Crystal Palmer, Safia Qurashi, Veronica Sanchis, Doreen Simon, Stephanie Traone, Iuliana Toma, Augustina Umokiwede, Sarah Wheeler, Emerson Vieira Gondin, Karen Whyte, Patricia Williams**

Marketing, Press and Box Office
Head of Marketing and Sales **Alix Hearn**
Press and Marketing Officer **Corinne O'Sullivan**
Marketing Officer **Tessa Gillett**
Box Office Manager **Angela Frost**

Box Office Supervisor **Beryl Warner**
Box Office Assistants **Asha Bhatti, Ana Gizelda Burke, Julie Lee, Stella Odunlami, Kemisha Plummer, Sarah Wheeler**

Production
Head of Stage **Simon Godfrey**
Head of Electrics **Kyle Macpherson**
Deputy Head of Electrics **George Dives**
Wardrobe Manager **Korinna Roeding**
Company and Stage Manager **Sarah Buik**

Front of House and Bar Staff
Bar and Front of House Manager **Leanda Linton**
Duty Managers **Nana Agyei, Danai Mavunga, Jenine Nelson, Rameeka Parvez**
Head Ushers **Akosua Acheampong, Rosie Christian, Tanoh Danson, Bradley Peter**
Ushers **Emma Choudhury, Rita Choudhury, Samantha Fink, Leeam Francis, Joan Kugonzo, Niharika Mahandru, Christine Matando, Doreen Ngozi, Reiss Nelson, Antonia Odunlami, Crystal Palmer, Razaam Parvez, Jordanna Phillips, Joshua Raheem, Magdalena Sobczynska, Sophie Tuitt, Nicholas Underwood, Heather Walker, Andrew Wright**
Fire Marshalls **Akosua Acheampong, Tanoh Danson, Charles Leanson, Rameeka Parvez**
Bar Supervisors **Leighton Lewis, Rameeka Parvez**, Benjamin Peter
Bar Team Leader **Michelle Scannell**
Bar Staff **Sabrina Alexander, Kieron Branch, Jackson Britton, Junior Buckley, Berengere Ariaudo De Castelli, Dwayne Hutchinson, Jowita Katarzyna, Daisy Lamb, Mutsa Mandeya, Roger McMlenaghan, Melanie Mesa, Crystal Palmer, Bradley Peter, Charlene Pierre, Joshua Raheem, Matt Widdowson**

Domestic Assistants **Denise Blake, Rehema Nyange, Kassim Ukware**
Board of Directors
Sally Banks, Sarah Isted (Treasurer), Derek Joseph, Jo Melville, Paul O'Leary (Chair), Mark Pritchard, Jane Storie.

Professional Advisors
Legal **Neil Adleman at Harbottle & Lewis LLP**
Insurance **Linda Potter at Giles Insurance Brokers Ltd**
Auditors **Kingston Smith**
Development **Sarah Mansell at Mansell Bouquet Ltd**

Please Support Us
All this amazing work costs money and we need your help! Theatre
Royal Stratford East is a charity. Box office income and funding from
our partners – Arts Council England, London Borough of Newham
and London Councils – covers only 85% of our costs, so every year
we need to raise an additional £375, 000. Please will you consider
supporting our work onstage or our inspirational programme for
young people and the wider community? You could even commission
a piece of new work, sponsor a production or youth project, join our
business club or simply make a donation.

Every little bit helps
Here are some of the ways you can help us:
Make a donation towards our *Young People's Work* and support the
work with young people, enabling them to explore the challenges they
face, share their stories and uncover hidden talent.
Become a member of our *Vision Collective* and support emerging
artists and new work. See our work 'from the inside' – benefits include
a newsletter, invitations to briefings, rehearsals and workshops.
Join our *Green Room Club* and promote your business, entertain
clients, reward and retain your staff. It is great fun and benefits include
advertising, branding, business-to-business networking, hospitality,
complimentary tickets and discounts.
Name a Seat and have a plaque with your inscription displayed on the
seat.
Leave a Legacy to the Joan Littlewood Fund and by leaving us a gift
in your Will, you are ensuring that future generations will continue to
enjoy the magic of Theatre Royal.
For further information on all sponsorships, donations, memberships
and legacies, please contact Emma Louise Norton on 020 8279 1138
or elnorton@stratfordeast.com.
Registered Charity No: 233801

We would like to thank the following for their support
With thanks to our funding partners

Trusts and Foundations
ACT Foundation, Children in Need, the Follett Trust, Jack Petchey
Foundation, Paul Hamlyn Foundation, Newham's Youth Opportunity
Fund and Find Your Talent.

Major Donors
Martina Cole, Elizabeth and Derek Joseph, Tony Hall CBE, Tony
Langham and Clare Parsons and all those who wish to remain
anonymous.

The Vision Collective

Sally Banks, Derek Brown, Barbara Ferris, Hachette UK, Tony Hall CBE, Elizabeth and Derek Joseph, Mansell Bouquet Ltd, Murray Melvin, Dr Stefano Nappo, Derek Paget, Toni Palmer, Bernard Richmond, Scrutton Estates Ltd, Gordon Sheret, Jan and Bill Smith, Dr Caryn Solomon, Jane Storie, Hedley G Wright, Sue Wyatt and all those who wish to remain anonymous.

Business Supporters

The Adam Street Private Members Club, Barclays Wealth, Birkbeck University of London, Clifford Chance LLP, East London Cars, Express by Holiday Inn London-Stratford, Harbottle & Lewis LLP, Lend Lease, London City Airport, JP Morgan, Tate & Lyle Sugars and Westfield Shopping Towns Limited.

We would also like to say thank you to the Avis Bunnage Estate, Peter Clayton and Richard Radcliffe for their support.

Contacting Theatre Royal Stratford East

Theatre Royal Stratford East, Gerry Raffles Square
London, E15 1BN
e-mail **theatreroyal@stratfordeast.com**
www.stratfordeast.com

Administration **020 8534 7374**
Fax **020 8534 8381**
Booking Line **020 8534 0310**
Box Office open **Mon to Sat, 10am – 6pm**
Press Direct Line **020 8279 1120**

We are delighted to take Typetalk calls, or if you prefer send us a text on **07972 918 050.**

Principal Funders

Pioneer Theatres Limited

VAT Number **248 9343 27**
Registration Number **556251**
Charity Number **233801**

TAKEAWAY

or THE DEVIL IN TOM JONES

Book and Lyrics by Robert Lee
Music by Leon Ko

TAKEAWAY

or THE DEVIL IN TOM JONES

A Musical

OBERON BOOKS
LONDON

WWW.OBERONBOOKS.COM

First published in 2011 by Oberon Books Ltd
521 Caledonian Road, London N7 9RH
Tel: +44 (0) 20 7607 3637 / Fax: +44 (0) 20 7607 3629
e-mail: info@oberonbooks.com
www.oberonbooks.com

A catalogue record for this book is available from the British
Library.

ISBN: 978-1-84943-208-5

Cover Photo: Robert Day
Cover design: n9design.com

Printed in Great Britain by CPI Antony Rowe, Chippenham.

For Michael and 'Ding'.

And for our parents, without whom none of this
would be necessary.

The creation of this show would not have been possible without the support, encouragement and input of the following individuals. They also happen to be some of the most generous, genuine and thoroughly remarkable souls you're likely to find. To every one of you: thank you.

Jonathan Bernstein, Fred Carl, Julianne Wick Davis, Donna DiNovelli, Mindi Dickstein, Randall Eng, Martin Epstein, Rob Hartmann, Danny Larsen, Mel Marvin, Sybille Pearson, Sarah Schlesinger

The faculty and students of the NYU Tisch School of the Arts Graduate Musical Theatre Writing Program

Donna Cain, Fay Ann Lee, BD Wong

Larry and Barbara Deal, Michael Deal, Tyan Yuan and Yen Yen Lee

Ed Durante, Clint Dyer, Karen Fisher, Philip Hedley, Robert Hyman, Kerry Michael, Rita Mishra, Dawn Reid, Ryan Romain, Ultz, Matthew 'Excalibah' Xia

Stephen Law, Rebecca Pan

Stephen Hoo, Sophiya Haque, Daryl Kwan, Pik-sen Lim, Craig Storrod, Shelley Williams, Gabby Wong

And last but by no means least,
the original cast and company of *Takeaway*

Authors' Note

There is an old saw that goes, 'Musicals are not written, but rewritten'. There is another that runs something along the lines of 'Musicals are not written, but abandoned'. Well, we're not quite ready for the 'abandonment' yet... But as of this writing, Boy Howdy are we deep into rewrites.

Writing an original musical is one of the most gratifying and masochistic experiences I know. Not only are the writers constantly chasing after – and being chased by – the Great Story Monster, the bulk of their creative time is spent imagining an entire world in a vacuum, without the invaluable points of reference provided by actors, directors, choreographers, musical directors, musicians and designers. As a result, what works on paper inevitably spins off into entropy as soon as it enters the province of those essential collaborators. With any luck, it all comes back together in the end. But for a brief, shining moment, the whole thing's a big, glorious mess.

Which brings me to the draft you hold in your hands, the rehearsal draft of *Takeaway* as of 24 May 2011. It is our hope the reader will approach it not as a finished product, but as a glimpse into the creative process: a snapshot taken midway through the rehearsal process, in those heady days when the characters are first becoming flesh and blood in the hands of an incredibly talented cast and creative team.

By the time you are reading this, there are portions of this script which will no doubt cause us some degree of embarrassment. Dialogue and lyrics – perhaps entire scenes – will have been changed or excised, important themes reinforced, obscure moments clarified, lame jokes sharpened or dropped. But what is here is the spirit of the piece, in full force.

So thank you for your indulgence, thank you for reading, and enjoy the hot mess.

Robert Lee,
Stratford, London
24 May 2011

Characters

EDDIE, 21, British-born Chinese
DILLON, 21, British Asian
LUM, 30s, Chinese
HENRY, 50, Chinese
ANGELA, 22, British-born Chinese
SHEILA, 25, Black British
REESE, 21, Caucasian
WIDOW CHU, 50s, Chinese
GUARDIAN ANGEL, ageless

LITTLE TOM JONES
TOM JONES' MOTHER
TWO FOREMEN
BACKUP SINGERS
LITTLE EDMOND WOO
EDMOND WOO'S MOTHER
BACKUP SINGERS
POSTAL WORKER
CASHIER
CHINESE GROCER
DOORMAN
PUB PATRONS
OFF-PITCH R&B SINGER
CONTEST STAFF MEMBER
PASTOR
SHEILA'S CO-WORKER
ELDER BROTHER
PHOTOGRAPHER
PASSENGER
FRIEND
CONDUCTOR

TIME: AUGUST 2011.

PLACE: EAST LONDON.

MUSICAL NUMBERS

ACT ONE

1. 'Take Me' *(Eddie, Backup Singers)*

2. 'A Woman's Touch' *(Eddie, Backup Singers, Angela, Sheila)*

3. 'Goldenballs' *(Reese, Eddie, Pub Patrons)*

4. 'Me and My Son' *(Henry)*

5. 'Chinaman's Chance' *(Eddie, Lum)*

6. 'Who is to Blame?' *(Angela, Reese, Dillon, Sheila, Lum)*

7. 'Before Love' *(Sheila, Angela, Dillon)*

8. 'Sing Your Song' *(Eddie, Company)*

9. 'The New Chinese Tom Jones' *(Dillon, Eddie, Reese, Company)*

ACT TWO

10. 'The Funeral' *(Mourners, Lum, Angela, Sheila)*

11. 'Eddie Woo/Come With' *(Eddie, Reese)*

12. 'Baby, We Can Lie All Night' *(Eddie, Sheila, Angela, Dillon)*

13. 'Yellow Power' *(Angela, Sheila, Elder Brother, Eddie, Militant Chorus)*

14. 'Come With' (Reprise) *(Eddie, Dillon)*

15. 'When I Sing' *(Widow Chu)*

16. 'A Divine Intervention' *(Guardian Angel)*

17. 'What Makes an Eddie Woo?' *(Eddie)*

18. Finale/Curtain Call *(Company)*

PROLOGUE

(Pre-show: the curtain is up. As the audience enters, it sees the interior of a Chinese takeaway. There is a door on one end leading outside and one on the other end leading to the kitchen. A third leads up to the flat upstairs. A sign overhead reads 'Happy Family' in weathered red and gold lettering.

There is a counter in front of the kitchen doorway, on which sits a cash register, an old Laughing Buddha in mahogany [or mahogany-coloured resin – it's hard to tell] and a jar of individually-wrapped fortune cookies, in addition to the normal takeaway accoutrements.

Vintage Tom Jones recordings from the '60s and '70s should be playing, as licensing fees permit.

As the show begins, the Tom Jones recordings are cut off abruptly by a flourish from the orchestra. EDDIE, a bespectacled British Chinese lad of 21, enters. He steps forward and recites, a Wikipedia entry in human form.)

EDDIE: Sir Thomas John Woodward, OBE, was born 7 June 1940 in Trefforest, Pontypridd, near Cardiff in Wales. He is particularly known for his powerful voice and overt sexuality. Since the mid-1960s he has sung nearly every form of popular music: pop, rock, R&B, show tunes, country, dance, techno and gospel. Since 1965 he has sold over 150 million records. He is better known by his stage name, Tom Jones.

(Beat.)

Edmond Woo was born 16 August 1990 in the London Borough of Newham. He is particularly known for his devotion to the music of Sir Thomas John Woodward, OBE. Since 2007 Woo has been assistant manager of his father's takeaway shop on Stratford High Street: 'Happy Family: High Quality Food, Low Quality Prices'. He has sold no records, won no prizes, and has no future prospects. But don't count him out just yet…

#1   **Take Me**   **(Eddie, Backup Singers)**

(Lights change and the takeaway set disappears as EDDIE continues. As he speaks, he removes his glasses and transforms before our eyes into the super-confident, ultra-sexy, hyper-masculine spitting image of his idol.)

… 'cos when it comes to croonin' 'n' spoonin', and flirtin' 'n' hurtin', and lustin' 'n' thrustin', and makin' you feel allllll the things a woman ought to feel…

(Singing out a WOMAN in the audience.)

Baby, I know *you're* feelin' all the things a woman ought to feel… 'Cos when a woman's feelin' all the things a woman ought to feel, she gets this glow in her 'special place'.

(Singing out another WOMAN in the audience.)

Mmmm! You know where that 'special place' is, don't you, baby!

(And another.)

I know *you* do!

(And another.)

And *you*!

(And another.)

And – baby, I'm not sure about you, why don't you open up and show me if you –

(All of a sudden shielding his eyes.)

whoa!!! A *blindin'* light! I seen it! I seen the light! The lady knows of what I speak! 'Cos when it comes to crooningandspooningandflirtingandhurtingandlusting andthrustingandmakingawomanfeel allllll the things a woman ought to feel, I know a thing or two.

And it goes a little something like this…

(Lights up on the rest of the stage. EDDIE stands on a concert stage, perhaps backed by the orchestra. To either side of him are risers seating an audience of SCREAMING FEMALE FANS. His BACKUP SINGERS are close by, executing some late sixties/ early seventies choreography when they're not singing.

EDDIE launches into a brassy, bombastic, rhythmic number that is vintage Tom Jones.)

What would you say to romance every day?
Go on, take me!
How would you feel 'bout a man makes you squeal?
Go on, take me!
A man's gotta do what a man's gotta do,
And all that this man's gotta do, babe, is you!
I'm made for the love, 'cos my last name is 'Woo'!

(Spoken.)

So how about it, baby?
Ow!!!!!

(Sung.)

Don't need a guide, yeah, I know what's inside –
Go on, take me!
I'll leave you numb, like I did to your mum!
Go on, take me!
The guys that you prize may be whiter 'n snow,
But swear that you care, and bye-bye, Romeo – !
Now, me, I don't leave, I got nowhere to go…

(Spoken.)

Except into your dreams, baby…
So you just sleep tight –
Ow!!!!!

(Sung.)

Take me, take me!

Take me, take me!
Take me, take me!
Take me take me take me take me…
Take me, take me!
Take me, take me!
Take me, take me!
Takemetakemetakemetakemetakemetakemetakeme
Take me!
Won't you take me…?

(Out, reverting suddenly to his normal persona.)

When he was twelve, Tom caught tuberculosis and spent two years in bed recovering. He said it was the worst time in his life. All he could do was listen to music and draw…

(LITTLE TOM JONES rolls on in a bed. His MOTHER enters from another direction.)

LITTLE TOM JONES: Mummy, may I go outside with the other boys to play Cnapan, a traditional Welsh game of medieval football?

TOM JONES' MOTHER: Thomas John Woodward, you may certainly not. Must I remind you you have tuberculosis? Now lie down and draw while I put on some music.

EDDIE: Later on, after he got married, he worked in a glove factory and then in construction.

(TWO FOREMEN enter and face out.)

TWO FOREMEN: Oi, Woodward! You call this stitching/brick-laying?

EDDIE: I guess that's why I feel such a strong connection – I mean, as a British-born Chinese.

(LITTLE EDMOND WOO rolls on at his desk. His MOTHER enters from another direction.)

LITTLE EDMOND WOO: Mummy, may I go outside with the other boys to play Uppies and Downies, a traditional English game of medieval football?

EDMOND WOO'S MOTHER: *(In a strong accent.)* Edmond Woo, you may certainly not. Must I remind you are Chinese? Now sit down and study your maths while I put on the Mandarin instructional tapes!

(LITTLE TOM JONES, his MOTHER, the FOREMEN, LITTLE EDMOND WOO and his MOTHER exit.)

EDDIE: He's living proof that no matter your roots, you too can grow up to become a Vegas legend, host of your own American television variety show, and the blackest white man in show business – no matter *what* your affliction!

(Back to his Tom Jones persona.)

Give me a try, I'll be bold, I'll be shy,

Go on, take me!

BACKUP SINGERS: Take me!

EDDIE: Leather or tweed, I'll be just what you need –
Go on, take me!

BACKUP SINGERS: Take me!

EDDIE: I'll wear me a vest and I'll get a tattoo –
I'll smash any test any girl ever threw –
No hair on my chest, 'cos I'm not from the zoo...

(Spoken.)

But that don't mean I'm not a beast, baby!
Huh!

(Sung.)

Don't be took in by the shade of my skin,
Go on, take me!
Don't be perplexed, 'cos you're soon to be sexed!
Can you take me?
Oh, let's get it on, baby, sloth is a vice –
I'm not bein' crude, I'm just bein' concise...
'Cos rice can be nice when it's covered in spice!

(Spoken.)

You get what I'm talkin' about?
Yeah!!!!!

EDDIE, BACKUP SINGERS: *(Sung.)* Take me, take me!
Take me, take me!
Take me, take me!
Take me take me take me take me...
Take me, take me!
Take me, take me!
Take me, take me!
Takemetakemetakemetakemetakemetakemetakemetakeme
Take me...!

EDDIE: *(Plain old 'EDDIE' once more.)* No doubt you're thinking: why
should an impressionable twenty-first century East London youth
be into Tom Jones? Thing is, we British East Asians – or whatever
we're calling ourselves – we're not very cool. Seriously, we're about
as 'street' as the M4 to Swindon. 'Cool', 'hip', 'sexy': we're wound
too tight. Nature or nurture, it just doesn't work. But 'sex' – pure,
unadulterated, no-nonsense, Tom Jones animal-style sex... 'Sex'
we can do! You doubt it, look at the population of China, the only
country in the world had to pass a law to stop people from doing the
nasty. And it wasn't 'cos they were busy listening to Engelbert bloody
Humperdinck!

(A blast from the orchestra and he is 'Tom Jones' once more, bringing it home.)

What will it be, baby, coffee or tea?
Go on, take me!

BACKUP SINGERS: Take me!

EDDIE: I wouldn't lie: tell me no, I may cry!
Go on, take me!

BACKUP SINGERS: Take me!

EDDIE: A chink you may think is a man to ignore –
He's weak and a geek and a bit of a bore...
Well, girl, who's a freak when your bottom is sore – ?

(Spoken.)

And I don't mean from smacking it yourself...!

(Sung.)

Ohhhhhhhhhhhhh –

EDDIE, BACKUP SINGERS: Take me, take me!
Take me, take me!
Take me, take me!
Take me take me take me take me...
Take me, take me!
Take me, take me!
Take me, take me!
Take me take me take me take me...
Take me, take me!
Take me, take me!
Take me, take me!
Take me take me take me take me...
Take me, take me!
Take me, take me!
Take me, take me!
Takemetakemetakemetakemetakemetakemetakeme
Take me!

EDDIE: Won't you take me...?

BACKUP SINGERS: Take me!

EDDIE: Ow!!!!!

(Playoff as we transition back to the takeaway.)

ACT ONE

SCENE ONE

(Tuesday, 12:30pm.

EDDIE is berating LUM, the takeaway's stubborn, surly Chinese cook. Throughout, LUM speaks in Mandarin.)

LUM: Wo bu ming bai.

EDDIE: Now, I know you understand me; I've seen you watching telly…

LUM: Wo jiu shi bu ming bai!

EDDIE: *Paris Hilton's British Best Friend* – ?

(Silence.)

I've seen you!

LUM: Hnh!

EDDIE: *(Beat; to the audience.)* Lum hasn't been with us very long. My father hired him because they both speak Mandarin and most people in London speak Cantonese. Our old cook spoke Mandarin, but he went back for the Olympics and made a fortune selling rodent-on-a-stick in front of the Bird's Nest… He and my father escaped from China together during the Cultural Revolution. Lum? He's from the 'New China': the one where people are selfish and have no manners.

(To LUM.)

Look, I just need you to stop yelling at the customers, alright? We're in Britain, they're gonna order chips, yeah? That's why we offer them on the menu. This isn't bloody Shanghai…

LUM: Wo shi chong Beijing lai de! Sha gua!

EDDIE: *(Has no idea what LUM has just said.)* Right then, off you go.

LUM: *(Exiting, muttering to himself.)* Hai yao ting xiao hai de hua…! Ba ni de na hua er kan diao!

(Exits.)

EDDIE: *(To the audience.)* My parents tried to get me to learn Chinese. They spoke it exclusively around the house when I was a child, and I was apparently quite good at it until I started learning English in school. Later on, they sent away for a set of tapes from Taiwan that were supposed to teach you while you slept. But after three months all I could manage was 'I need to go to the bathroom. Where is the nearest bank?'

(Enter DILLON on her bike. She is a striking yet tomboyish 21-year-old Asian woman who handles the takeaway's delivery orders.)

DILLON: *(Horribly out of tune.)* Happy birthday dear Ed-die-e-e-e-e-e-… Happy birthday to you! Wooooo!

(Throws a pitifully spare handful of confetti in EDDIE's face.)

EDDIE: *(To the audience.)* Did I mention it's my birthday? Twenty-one. Milestone, innit. Though when you're Chinese, you're a year old at birth, which means you're already twelve months behind… Explains a lot, don't it?

DILLON: Hello, luv! All right?

EDDIE: *(Cheerful.)* Oh, handling the lunch rush by myself, trying to keep the cook from killing the customers… convincing the delivery orders that 'pick-up' is the better option…

DILLON: *(Parking her bike.)* That Lum's a loose cannon…!

EDDIE: He's on time.

DILLON: I'm always on time!

EDDIE: Just because you say it don't make it true.

(To the audience.)

Dillon is my oldest friend in the world and our takeaway's designated delivery person. Though she hasn't quite grasped the importance of popping in from time to time to – I don't know – pick up the orders.

(To DILLON.)

You wanna watch yourself. Dad's going mental.

DILLON: *(Glancing up to the flat above.)* You know what he needs –

EDDIE: *(Sweeping up his own birthday confetti.)* 'A good shag'. That's your answer to everything.

DILLON: You should try it sometime.

(Deep breath.)

So… today's the big day…!

EDDIE: You're not going to chuck anything else at me…

DILLON: I mean your A-level results. And on your twenty-first birthday! Oh, the irony… I mean, this being your last chance and all. Not that there's any pressure…!

EDDIE: Relax! I told you, I did really well this year.

DILLON: Has it come, then? The post?

EDDIE: Here any minute. How about that, for once you beat it in!

DILLON: How can you be so calm?

EDDIE: I'm telling ya, I studied this time – it's in the bag! Don't you believe me?

DILLON: Honestly, with you I never know *what* to think.

EDDIE: Well, if you were so concerned, you could have come in before lunch, instead of morning croissants with 'Del-roy'.

DILLON: I wasn't with Delroy... or Panni.

EDDIE: Who's Panni?

DILLON: Keep up, there are only ever two at any one time. I was practicing.

(Produces a folded handbill from under her blouse. EDDIE handles it gingerly.)

EDDIE: *(Reading from the handbill.)* 'Britain's Newest Unexpected Singing Sensation'!

DILLON: I picked it up when I was delivering to that music studio by the job centre. It's a talent competition/reality show. Winner gets a recording contract and a yearlong concert tour!

EDDIE: 'Voices of gold – from the people you'd least suspect...'?

DILLON: Cab drivers, computer scientists... delivery women! Trying to capitalize on the whole Susan Boyle thing, innit? Honestly, if *that* shabby lot can do it...

EDDIE: But darling... you don't sing!

DILLON: I do, too!

EDDIE: Not to mention your stage fright. Remember the Newham Town Show...? You stood there like an idiot for ten minutes with the music playing.

DILLON: You're mean. I was only five!

(Snatching the handbill from him.)

You know your problem, Eddie? You haven't got any courage. Or conviction. Or imagination.

EDDIE: Not true.

DILLON: So why you still here, then? Living at home, working in your father's takeaway for no pay, half ten to midnight, three hundred sixty-five days a year...

EDDIE: It's just temporary! All that's going to change –

DILLON: – once you pass your A-levels, I know.

EDDIE: That's right!

DILLON: Well, if I can stand by you after three years of failed A-levels, you can support me in my bid for super-stardom. First round's Thursday, at The Flying Nanny, after work.

EDDIE: What, that karaoke bar 'round the corner from Jewson's?

DILLON: Bringing the contest to the people! Prepare to be astonished. Gonna be my moral support.

EDDIE: Karaoke!

DILLON: We'll go there tonight, for birthday drinks. Plus, I've got a surprise for you!

EDDIE: I don't know…

(The bell on the front door rings. EDDIE and DILLON grab each other's hand as a POSTAL WORKER enters with a stack of mail and an electronic clipboard.)

POSTAL WORKER: Sign.

(EDDIE signs the clipboard nervously, hands it back.)

Cheers…

(Winking.)

And could I have a number 69, please?

(Exits.

EDDIE and DILLON look at each other, then at the letter at the top of the stack of mail.)

DILLON: Is it – ?

EDDIE: It is. Look at it.

DILLON: It's like… Evil.

(They both glance upstairs in the direction of the flat. EDDIE hurriedly sets the rest of the stack on the counter.)

Openitopenitopenit…!

EDDIE: Hold on – I want to savour this moment…

DILLON: Scared?

(Beat.)

EDDIE: Not in the slightest.

(He is.)

DILLON: Fourth time's a charm…

(EDDIE begins to open the letter.

As if willing it to happen.)

My boy's going to uni!

(We hear EDDIE's father HENRY coming down the stairs. EDDIE hands the letter to DILLON and she exits into the kitchen. We hear LUM bark at her from offstage.)

LUM: *(Offstage.)* Ey?! Shei shuo ni ke yi jing lai de!

(HENRY enters from upstairs as EDDIE picks up the rest of the mail.)

EDDIE: Dad…

HENRY: Ey, was that the post?

EDDIE: *(Showing him the stack of mail.)* Just some bills and catalogues.

HENRY: Nothing else?

(EDDIE shrugs.)

Did you fill out the address on the test – ?!

EDDIE: Yes!

(Beat.)

HENRY: You should call about your results, last year they come earlier.

EDDIE: Right.

HENRY: And where is that Dillon?! My friend, he calls, ordering the delivery – says the person on the phone tells him he should get the exercise! I tell you, these Indians never know how to talk with the customer. Any culture that will worship the cow? Bad people skill!

EDDIE: I'll have a talk with her.

HENRY: You are the assistant manager, this is your responsibility! This is why your mother and I, we told you to study…

EDDIE: You going out, then?

HENRY: Ah? Oh. Mmm. Have the important business…! You remember to order the new napkin, ah? Nothing cheaper than the takeaway without the napkin!

(Exits out the front door in a bluster.

A moment. DILLON emerges cautiously and slips the letter back to EDDIE.)

DILLON: *(Whispering.)* Right, on the count of three…! One, two…!

(EDDIE rips the envelope open and the two skim its contents.

Beat. DILLON looks at EDDIE.

Disappointed.)

Oh, Eddie…

(EDDIE just stares at the letter.

Beat.

#2   A Woman's Touch   (Eddie, Backup Singers, Angela, Sheila)

Lights change abruptly. EDDIE turns to the audience, in 'performance mode' once more – cool, in control and dripping with sex.)

EDDIE: *(To the audience.)* Said my mama, 'There'll be days, my son,
When this world is like a hit-and-run…
When the friend you always trusted lied
And your favourite little guppy died…'
Said my mama, 'On a day like such,
What you need is a woman's touch!'

(Lights fade on DILLON and the takeaway.

To the audience.)

When he was sick in bed with TB, it was Tom's Mum who mainly pulled him through... she and thoughts of the lively eleven year-old neighbourhood girl destined to become his future wife. These two became the first in a long line of select women who would help see him through rough times. One estimate put their number at around ten thousand. Me, I'm sort of a late bloomer: I'm only on number six... and-a-half.

(Sung.)

Said my mama, ''Cos a woman's thang
Is to help a fella "yin" his "yang".
Yeah, a woman always "understands" – '
And she know just where to put her hands...!
Said my mama, 'When you feel too much,
Boy, it's time for a woman's touch!'
All right! Hey, hey!

BACKUP SINGERS: *(Appearing.)* It's a woman's touch...

EDDIE: Little darlin'...!

BACKUP SINGERS: Just a woman's touch...

EDDIE: Sing it to me, baby – !

BACKUP SINGERS: Yes, a woman's touch...

EDDIE: That's what she told me!

BACKUP SINGERS: Bless a woman's touch...

EDDIE: I wanna do you proud, Mama – !

BACKUP SINGERS: Trust a woman's touch...

EDDIE: Give it to me one more time!

BACKUP SINGERS: Just a woman's –

EDDIE: Owwww!

(Segue to:)

SCENE TWO

EDDIE: *(To the audience.)* My own experience with women began about a month after Mum's funeral, with a girl who approached me in the Oriental Foods section of Sainsbury's. One minute we were eyeing each other over the Wing Yip Super Grade Oyster Sauce, the next we were making sloppy stir-fry in her deep cast-iron wok. But it was enough to unlock for me one of the great secrets of the Universe. 'Cos though you won't hear it talked about in decent company, there's nothing gets you hard-*up* like a proper let*down*.

(EDDIE gestures. Tight spot on the clock on the wall, which speeds forward to three o'clock in the afternoon, as if by the force of his will. He puts a 'We'll be back at five

o'clock' sign up in the front window and steps forward as the takeaway set disappears once again. To the audience.)

Now, a man may make a million friends,
Every one a homo sapiens;
Still it's all a load a' gobbl'ygook
If he doesn't get that nookie-nook...!
Said my mama, 'Gotta pop that clutch,
And go find you a woman's touch!'
'Cos a woman with an iron grip,
Will erase that old rejection slip.
And a woman with a velvet glove...
Honey, that's a little thing called 'love'!
Said my mama, 'We all need a crutch –
So make time for a woman's touch!'
That's right! That's what she said!

BACKUP SINGERS: Get a woman's touch...

EDDIE: Oh, baby...!

BACKUP SINGERS: Yeah, a woman's touch...

EDDIE: Go out there and take it – !

BACKUP SINGERS: Grab a woman's touch...

EDDIE: Rope it in like a heifer!

BACKUP SINGERS: Fab, a woman's touch...

EDDIE: I like it when you fight me – !

BACKUP SINGERS: Wild, a woman's touch...

EDDIE: Oh, mercy – !

BACKUP SINGERS: Child, a woman's –

EDDIE: Owwww!

(EDDIE faces out and mimes pushing a button. We hear a buzz and ANGELA, a defiant young British Chinese woman of 22, steps forward in a spotlight.

The following scenes are played out to the audience, in abstraction.)

ANGELA: Eddie! You're early!

EDDIE: *(Suggestive, though awkwardly so.)* Easy, baby; you know I never come too soon!

ANGELA: Mmmm!

(They begin to undress.)

EDDIE: *(To the audience.)* Angela I met online, through her East Asian empowerment website, www.takethatevilwhiteman.org. She's got everything: looks, brains, and a sureness about herself that's – well, borderline terrifying...

ANGELA: *(In coitus, her eyes shut tight.)* Who's a powerful East-Asian man?!

EDDIE: I am!

ANGELA: Who's a powerful East-Asian man?!?!

EDDIE: I am!!

ANGELA: Who's a powerful East-Asian man?!?!?!

EDDIE: *I AM*!!!

(To the audience.)

Twice a week, at three-fifteen on the dot, we get together and bond over ownership initiatives and oppression theory.

ANGELA: Take me by force, my Yellow Stallion!

EDDIE: Did I mention she thinks I'm a law student specializing in cases of cultural bias and institutionalised racism?

(ANGELA lets out a gasp of excitement.)

Sometimes she inspires me to change the world. Other times I just focus on her breasts. Either way, for forty-five minutes it's the New Yellow Order, and we are its masters.

ANGELA: Eddie, Eddie, Eddie,
Do it hard and rough.
I'm your little piggy;
Go on, huff and puff!
Never met a Brother
Who could turn me on…
I'll be Central Asia,
You be Genghis Khan.
Eddie, Eddie, Eddie,
Where'd you get that strut?
Make me guess your colour
When my eyes are shut…!
Eddie, Eddie, Eddie,
Won't you take me now – ?
Liberate my countryside
Like Chairman Mao!
Let my oriental mama
Scowl and say,
'Boys and girls in China
Aren't made that way!'
Eddie, Eddie, Eddie,
Make me writhe and bounce,
Show me it's the motion,
Not the size that counts!

(The onstage clock speeds forward to 4:15.

SHEILA, black and 25, appears on the other side of EDDIE, wearing a Chinese print. She is in a different time and place from ANGELA, and so does not acknowledge her.)

EDDIE: *(To the audience.)* Sheila and I first met at the HMV on High Street. I was looking for Tom Jones' 'Something 'Bout You Baby I Like', she was looking for '40 Buddhist Chants to Live By'. It was True Love at the Bargain Bin.

SHEILA: *(Chanting.)* Na mo he la da na duo la ye ye…

EDDIE: *(To the audience.)* Sheila's the assistant at the Public Library and is positively transported by anything foreign: food, clothes, music, people. Lucky for her, I happen to be heir to the throne of an obscure island nation somewhere in the China Sea…

SHEILA: Talk dirty to me, Eddie… in the language of your people…

EDDIE: Sheila's a person with love for all the peoples of the world. All, that is, except for one…

SHEILA: When will black people realise that Morgan Freeman *cannot hear them through the bloody screen*?!

EDDIE: I might point out that this is rather intolerant behaviour for a Buddhist, but truth be told, the whole thing kind of freaks me out!

SHEILA: *(To EDDIE, in very bad Mandarin and gesturing as if to a deaf person.)* Ni shi wo qing ai de ren!

(Now in the present day; to EDDIE.)

Eddie! I didn't think we were meeting today…

EDDIE: *(Incongruously.)* Easy, baby; you know I never come too soon!

SHEILA: *(Sniffs at the air.)* Is that a new soap?

EDDIE: *(Panicking a bit, sniffing himself.)* Would you like me to shower?

SHEILA: No, I like it! Is it something from home?

EDDIE: Sort of…

(To the audience.)

Angela's…!

SHEILA: Well, I like it!

(Savouring the smell.)

Spice, from the Orient!

EDDIE: Cheers…

SHEILA: Maybe next time you can bring a bottle and we can douse the sheets!

EDDIE: *(Playing the helpless innocent.)* What means 'douse'?

SHEILA: *(This last has clearly turned her on; undressing and spreading her legs.)* Mmmm! Let me show you…!
Black is lazy and white's too fast…
Need a yellah man to make it last – !

Go slow – !
Ooh, Eddie, baby, go slow, now…!
Oh, show me a love respectful and true,
And all the kinky things that your people do – !
Go slow,
Ooh, Eddie, baby, go slow, now…!
Do it slow as the district line –
Let me be your *Favourite Concubine…*
Slow – !
Ooh, steady, baby, below, now…!
Oh, teach me some words in Chinese or Thai…
I won't ask too much because you're so shy…
We'll be the sequel to *The King and I* – !
Go slow, Eddie, baby, go slow!

(Beat as EDDIE takes both of them in appreciatively. He gives the audience a devilish look.)

EDDIE: And a-one, two, three, four – !

(EDDIE plunges in and begins making love to them both as all three sing.)

SHEILA, ANGELA, BACKUP SINGERS: Ooh! A woman's touch…

EDDIE: Sing it with me, darlin'!

SHEILA, ANGELA, BACKUP SINGERS: Uh! A woman's touch…

EDDIE: I'll be anything you desire, baby!

SHEILA, ANGELA, BACKUP SINGERS: Oh! A woman's touch…

EDDIE: It's you and me against the world, honey!

SHEILA, ANGELA, BACKUP SINGERS: Ah! A woman's touch…

EDDIE: A little louder, I can't quite hear ya, now –

SHEILA, ANGELA, BACKUP SINGERS: Nnnh! A woman's touch…

EDDIE: Baby, move your arm a little to the side there, won't ya?

SHEILA, ANGELA, BACKUP SINGERS: Huh! A woman's –

EDDIE: Mmmmmm!

(Spoken.)

Now, I realise some might call me a cheat… a liar… a fake… But long as I keep my facts straight, everyone stays happy. Angela gets her Yellow Warrior. Sheila gets her Foreign Prince. All it takes is a little bit of distance and a great alibi.

ANGELA: I would sooo love it if you could come to my Rally for the Victims of the 2004 Morecambe Bay Cockling Disaster!

SHEILA: I would sooo love for you to meet my Racial Encounter Group at the library!

EDDIE: *(To ANGELA and SHEILA, respectively.)* Sorry, darling, I've got class Friday afternoon… Sorry, love, Friday's my luncheon with my father, the King.

(To the audience.)

It's a bit like those lads freerunning all over the South Bank: one slip and 'splat', in front of everyone and their dog. But while you're flying – there ain't a thing you can't do.

SHEILA: Longer!

ANGELA: Harder!

SHEILA: Slower!

ANGELA: Faster!

(The requests get more insistent as it becomes clear EDDIE is not performing up to his normal standard.)

SHEILA: Longer!

ANGELA: Harder!

SHEILA: Slower!

ANGELA: Faster!

SHEILA, ANGELA: *(Chanted, double-time.)* Longer,
Harder,
Slower,
Faster,
Longer,
Harder,
Slower,
Faster,
Longer,
Harder,
Slower,
Faster –

EDDIE, SHEILA, ANGELA: *(Chanted.)* Faster, faster, faster, faster – !

(During the following, EDDIE works up an increasing sweat trying to service the women, his thrusts getting more aggressive and desperate.)

SHEILA, ANGELA, BACKUP SINGERS: *(Sung.)* It's a woman's touch…

EDDIE: See ya later, napkin orders!

SHEILA, ANGELA, BACKUP SINGERS: Yes, a woman's touch…

EDDIE: Farewell, disappointed fathers…!

SHEILA, ANGELA, BACKUP SINGERS: Praise a woman's touch…

EDDIE: Bye-bye homicidal chef-man…!

SHEILA, ANGELA, BACKUP SINGERS: Bless a woman's touch…

EDDIE: Don't need no twenty-first birthday party…!

SHEILA, ANGELA, BACKUP SINGERS: Hail a woman's touch…

EDDIE: In a while, Mister A-level…!

SHEILA, ANGELA, BACKUP SINGERS: Frail, A woman's touch…

EDDIE: Owwww!

(HENRY, LUM and DILLON appear in individual spotlights.)

HENRY: *(To EDDIE.)* This is why your mother and I, we told you to study – !

EDDIE: UM –

SHEILA, ANGELA, BACKUP SINGERS: A woman's touch…

LUM: *(To EDDIE.)* Ba ni de na hua er kan diao – !

EDDIE: Right –

SHEILA, ANGELA, BACKUP SINGERS: A woman's touch …

DILLON: *(To EDDIE.)* – And on your twenty-first birthday!

EDDIE: Yeah, funny that!

SHEILA, ANGELA, BACKUP SINGERS: A woman's touch …

EDDIE: *(Distracted.)* … Two, three, four – !

(HENRY, LUM and DILLON remain lit – and in EDDIE's mind – for the following.)

SHEILA, ANGELA, BACKUP SINGERS: Get a woman's touch…

EDDIE: *(To ANGELA, with increasing frustration and desperation, as he finds he is unable to perform for the first time.)* Baby, don't move around so much, will ya?

SHEILA, ANGELA, BACKUP SINGERS: Yeah, a woman's touch…

EDDIE: *(To SHEILA, distracted.)* Wait, honey, let me do it myself…!

SHEILA, ANGELA, BACKUP SINGERS: Trust a woman's touch…

EDDIE: *(To ANGELA.)* Here, why don't you try getting on top –

SHEILA, ANGELA, BACKUP SINGERS: Just a woman's touch…

EDDIE: *(To SHEILA.)* Okay, bad idea…

SHEILA, ANGELA, BACKUP SINGERS: Swell, a woman's touch…

EDDIE: *(Making a colossal last-ditch effort – whatever he's done, it almost certainly hurt.)* Arrrrrrnnnggghhhh – !

(ANGELA and SHEILA stop as music drops to a steady, monotonous pulse. HENRY, LUM and DILLON disappear.)

ANGELA: *(Opening her eyes.)* Eddie…?

EDDIE: *(Wheezing.)* I'm alright! Just give me a moment.

ANGELA: Do you think maybe we should –

EDDIE: Naw, I'm fine! Just give me a moment…

SHEILA: Eddie, you're hyperventilating!

EDDIE: No, no, look! I'm good as new!

(An enormous gasp of air.)

… Just give me a moment…!

ANGELA: Eddie, it's alright:

(Music stops.)

SHEILA, ANGELA: *(Sympathetic but clearly disappointed.)* It happens to everyone.

(EDDIE looks out, frustrated.)

EDDIE: *(To the audience.)* Bloody hell – !

SHEILA, ANGELA, BACKUP SINGERS: *(Overlapping.)*

    – A woman's touch…!

    – A woman's touch…!

    – A woman's touch…!

EDDIE, SHEILA, ANGELA, BACKUP SINGERS: Gone to hell with a woman's touch!

(Blackout.)

SCENE THREE

(The Flying Nanny, a local pub, later that night. DILLON and EDDIE sit at a table. DILLON chatters away as EDDIE sits glumly.)

EDDIE: You need a what?

DILLON: Secret identity! You know, to help me when I perform!

EDDIE: What singer has a secret identity?!

DILLON: Beyoncé.

EDDIE: Who?

DILLON: Beyoncé! In real life, she's this innocent thing, but onstage she has this secret identity – 'Sasha Fierce' – and it's all sex, all of the time. Or Boy George…!

EDDIE: *(He's figured it out.)* You mean 'alter-ego'!

DILLON: Alter-what?

EDDIE: '-Ego,' '-ego'! It's called an 'alter-ego'.

(Beat.)

DILLON: I think I'd rather have a secret identity.

(EDDIE buries his face in his hands.)

Cheer up. Something will turn up. What about a BTech?

EDDIE: Have you *met* my father?

DILLON: Or take over the shop.

EDDIE: Have you met *me?*

DILLON: See, this is where a good shagging would come in handy…

EDDIE: Here, let me take a look at that leaflet, will you?

DILLON: What, for *Britain's Newest Unexpected Singing Sensation?*

(Hands it to him.)

You're not thinking of entering, are you? I mean, well… it'd get you out, but you haven't got any talent.

EDDIE: I'm just looking! Whatever happened to 'Have a little imagination'?

DILLON: Yeah, but let's not be ridiculous. Do you even listen to music? Hey, I've got a better idea: you can be my tour manager! 'Get me another G and T!'

(EDDIE gives her a look as if to say, 'You must be joking'. Getting up and taking his glass.)

Right. Be right back. Maybe I'll shake things up, bring you a Fat Coke.

(Sympathetic.)

Happy twenty-first, darling!

EDDIE: *(Calling after her.)* I'm still waiting for my surprise!

(To the audience.)

I don't know why everyone goes on about being twenty-one. I mean, you can get married at 16… drive a van at 17… the next year you're buying a round of drinks and voting. Far as I can tell, you can be a divorced Tory alcoholic in jail for vehicular manslaughter before your 19th birthday. Tom Jones was nearly twenty-five when he had his big break… and that almost didn't happen. See, his first hit record, 'It's Not Unusual,' was written for Sandie Shaw. Then when he did record it, the BBC wouldn't play it on account of it being too raunchy. If not for pirate radio, a lot of knickers might still be alive today. There's a lesson in all this: it's like the saying goes, 'A diamond's just a lump of coal that did well under pressure'. Or maybe, 'Impotence is a hard-on in search of inspiration'.

(Looks at the handbill. Taking the piss.)

Britain's Newest Unexpected Singing Sensation!
(Beat; defensive.)

I mean, stranger things have happened…

(There is a sudden crash of thunder as the door to the pub flies open to reveal REESE, 21 and one of the most gorgeous men you've ever seen. He carries a small rucksack over one shoulder, effortlessly.)

#3   **Goldenballs**   (Reese)

Oh, what – when it rains, it really bloody pours.

(Music begins as we are again in EDDIE's mind. REESE struts in, greeting various PUB PATRONS, almost unbearably cool and confident and flashing an irresistible smile.)

As if there weren't plenty of other reasons to hate this day! Reese Parker-Bennett made every moment of secondary school a living hell with his perfect grades and perfect teeth.

REESE: *(Spotting EDDIE; as if using an old, familiar nickname.)* Eddie 'Who?'

(Beat; chuckles at his own joke.)

EDDIE: It wasn't that he was ever cruel or unkind. No, Reese Parker-Bennett understood the mere fact of his existence was enough to make a mockery of mine.

REESE: You want fabulous smile,
You want devil-may-care,
You want what I got,
So, why not let me show it to ya?
You want colourful style,
You want glamorous hair,
You want beauty spot –
Well, I got six or seven for ya!
Anything your heart may desire,
You'll find in me –
And baby, endlessly.
I was put on earth to inspire –
I'm more than man,
I'm like a 'mantasy'!
(Spoken.)
That's like a 'fantasy', except… I'm a man – !
(Sung.)
I'm sexy, I'm gorgeous,
I do what I like.
My shirts are by Calvin,
My shoes are by Nike.
You heard about 'Goldenballs'?
Well, baby, I got 'em!
I'm cocky, I'm crazy,
I win every fight.
I'm late every morning,
'Cos I last all night!
I got me some Goldenballs…
Aw, baby, you'll like 'em!
Won't refuse me,
Can't resist me

Once you've kissed me –
That's the siren call
Of he with the Goldenballs!

REESE: You want –

EDDIE: 'Is his own man' …

REESE: You want –

EDDIE: 'Has his own flat'…

REESE: You want –

EDDIE: 'Paragon' …

REESE: Well, feast your eyes on heaven, baby…!

EDDIE: You want –

REESE: 'Luckier than'!

EDDIE: You want –

REESE: 'Really all that'!

EDDIE: You want –

REESE: 'Marathon'…?
My time is three oh-seven, baby!

PUB PATRONS: *(To EDDIE.)* Everything you try is a terrible tragedy –
It's, like, your destiny.
Hair that puffs and clothes barely wearable:
That's your lot…

REESE: Now, let's get back to me!
I'm rakish, I'm charming,
I run with the best.
I'm always the wanker
Who's partly undressed.
You wanna see Goldenballs?
Well, baby, I brought 'em…!
I'm cuddly, I'm manly,
I sure hit the spot!
I'm utter perfection,
I'm all that you're not…
I got me some Goldenballs,
And you're at the bottom…!
Don't resent me.
Don't deny me.
Compliment me.
Deify me.
Don't reject me
'Til you try me…
You can have it all –
Take me and my Goldenballs!

Goldenballs!
Golden Goldenballs!
… and my Goldenballs!
Goldenballs!

PUB PATRONS: *(Under the above.)*
He's sexy, he's gorgeous,
His life is a breeze.
He's cocky, he's crazy,
He's brilliant on skis.
He's rakish, he's charming,
He takes 'em in threes.
He's cuddly, he's manly,
We're down on our knees…
Ahhhh – !

DILLON: *(Spotting REESE from the bar.)*
Reese!

(Rushes to EDDIE at the table and hastily sets the drinks down.

To EDDIE.)

Here…

(Hurries back over to join REESE and escort him back to EDDIE.)

REESE: *(Seeing EDDIE for the first time.)* Eddie Woo! Alright?

DILLON: Eddie, you remember Reese Parker, from school?

(EDDIE instinctively removes his glasses.)

EDDIE: 'Parker-Bennett'.

REESE: No, it's just 'Parker' nowadays. 'Parker-Bennett''s a bit much.
Plus my father's a bit of a twat.

EDDIE: What are you doing here? Last I heard you were working for
that actress on telly.

DILLON: Reese is working on the show!

EDDIE: Show?

DILLON: Ran into him at the music studio. He was setting out the flyers.

REESE: Sort of an assistant to an assistant, but it's great, meeting all these
regular folk, making their dreams happen!

DILLON: *('Isn't that sweet?')* Aww!

REESE: *(To EDDIE, pointing at his handbill.)* Are you auditioning as well?

EDDIE: *(Handing the handbill to him by reflex.)* Wha – ? No! I'm not very
musical!

(DILLON takes it.)

REESE: Aw, that's too bad. 'Music washes away from the soul the dust of
everyday life'.

DILLON: That's nice…!

REESE: Yeah, it was on my screensaver.

DILLON: Reese is gonna help me prepare.

REESE: Yeah, 'checking the scene of the crime!'

EDDIE: You mean 'casing the joint'.

REESE: Hey, I get to give out tickets for the second round Saturday night, at the Scala. Want me to put you both on the list?

DILLON: What, in Soho? Wow!

REESE: That's the one that's gonna be on telly, live and everything.

(To DILLON.)

I mean, I'm sure you'll make the first round, but – just in case…

(To both.)

Show starts at half-seven…

EDDIE: We don't close until one.

REESE: Well, I'll put you down anyway… You still working at the takeaway then? Gonna be running the place, soon!

(The comment cuts EDDIE like a knife.

Putting his arm around DILLON. The effect on her is intoxicating.)

What about this one, eh? Who would have thought our Dillon would end up an actress?

(DILLON gives EDDIE a 'just go along with it' look.)

DILLON: Well… auditioning, anyway!

REESE: No, you're really doing it!

EDDIE: *(Pointed.)* Yeah, you're really doing it!

REESE: Look, I'm desperate for a slash – Tube, you know. I'll be right back! I can't believe it, the three of us here, after all these years… really going places!

(Exits.)

DILLON: I said I was at the studio for voice lessons – ! I couldn't tell him the truth… With him it's always something new and exciting!

EDDIE: You couldn't have said I was – I don't know, a vet?!

DILLON: *('Well, isn't that something?')* You want to be a vet?

(Beat.)

I meant to tell you when we sat down, honestly, but I forgot…

EDDIE: When we sat – wait, *him* – ? *Reese* – ? *That* was my surprise?

DILLON: I thought you liked him.

EDDIE: *You* liked him! I sat in front of him in Maths.

DILLON: Well, I'm sorry I got confused.

EDDIE: All through sixth form it was 'I wonder what Reese is doing? I wonder if Reese got my email. I wonder if Reese has seen *Slumdog Millionaire*?' You're bloody obsessed!

DILLON: I am not.

EDDIE: Besides, you're with Delroy now. And Panni.

DILLON: You're just jealous because he's gotten out and made something of himself.

EDDIE: Oh, right, an assistant to an assistant!

DILLON: *(Genuinely bewildered.)* You hate him. You really hate him. And him being so devastatingly beautiful. This is what I get for trying to throw my best friend a twenty-first birthday party!

EDDIE: Party? *Party?* You asked me out so I could be your *wingman*!

DILLON: That is so tacky!

EDDIE: I completely agree!

DILLON: I meant your pulling me up on it!

EDDIE: You know what? I'm gone.

DILLON: Come on, Eddie, I can't do this alone!

EDDIE: Sure you can, you're an actress!

DILLON: Don't be that way – !

(Obliviously encouraging.)

Look, just because you've bodged up your own life, don't mean you can't still help out with mine…!

EDDIE: Oh, thanks! Thanks a lot!

(To himself, waving his hands in the air in mock celebration.)

'Happy birthdayyyyyy!'

(Blows out the candles on an air-cake, then 'catches himself'.

'Silly me!')

No cake!

DILLON: Eddie –

(EDDIE gets up, just as REESE returns.)

REESE: *(To EDDIE.)* You going…?

EDDIE: Yeah, I've got work in the morning.

(Pointed, to DILLON.)

Not all of us are blessed with a future, you know!

(Exits.)

REESE: Well, am I gonna get to –

(But EDDIE has gone.

REESE and DILLON look at each other.)

SCENE FOUR

(We follow EDDIE as he leaves the pub and returns to the shop. Outside the door, he pulls out the letter containing his results.

A moment. He returns the letter to his pocket and unlocks the front door. He enters quietly.

The lights are off. There are two large widescreen flat panel TV sets in the room. The cardboard boxes in which they arrived are strewn about, along with other miscellaneous packing materials. Both sets have been left on. In their glow we can see HENRY asleep at the counter.

HENRY wakes.)

HENRY: Ah – ?

EDDIE: Sorry, Dad.

HENRY: It is so late!

EDDIE: I know, Dad, I went out with Dillon…

HENRY: That Dillon…!

EDDIE: I should have called –

HENRY: *(Groggy.)* If you are going to be late, you need to call!

EDDIE: I know…!

(Beat.)

What's with the tellies?

HENRY: *(Getting up excitedly, scrambling to sort out the remotes.)* Aw! Look, look…!

(He switches the two sets to the same channel, a nature program – perhaps 'Planet Earth'.)

Amazing, ah?

(Comparing the two screens.)

Would you say 'big difference', 'little difference', or 'medium difference'?

EDDIE: Um… 'No difference'?

HENRY: Ah?!

EDDIE: 'Little difference'!

HENRY: 'Little difference'?!

EDDIE: Well, they look like the same set to me…

HENRY: Because you are careless, never pay attention!

(At one screen, with vague disgust.)

This is 1080i…

(At the other, beaming.)

This is 1080p!

(Pointing at the screen.)

See the bubbles…? Wah, so advanced.

EDDIE: *(Humouring him.)* Oh, wait – yeah, I see now! 'Big difference'!

HENRY: *(Pleased.)* Really? Hwah! I would have said 'medium difference'!

EDDIE: Well, they're both high def, aren't they?

HENRY: *(Offended.)* No!

(Once more at the one screen, with vague disgust.)

One is 1080i…

(And at the other, beaming.)

One is 1080p! The better one we keep. Put it in the restaurant, let the customer watch the matches. Maybe later, you help me move them upstairs… What do you think, ah?

EDDIE: They're a bit large for the shop, aren't they?

HENRY: Ah?!

EDDIE: Well, yeah, I mean, there's no room –

HENRY: This is your problem, Edmond! Always think too small! Never have the ambition! Always want to be 'good enough'… When I take the test in the university, do you think I only try for the sixty percent? Try to be 'good enough'? I try for the one hundred percent! You have the food to eat, the – the Jaffa Cake, the place to live, this standard of living: you think you will have this if you only try to be 'good enough'? You will starve! You think all this is the automatic? No…! In university, even I am always number one, I do not have the mansion, I do not have the servant. Imagine if I am only the sixty percent? 'Good enough'… Why do you think you can afford take the A-level four times? In all the world, the hard work is the only thing you can control. Why do you want to be so stupid, give that up, ah? Ah?

(Beat.

Embarrassed at having lost his temper.)

Mmm. 'Take the A-level, take the A-level'. Even I am tired of hearing me say it…

(EDDIE smiles feebly.)

This is not what I want to stay up, talk to you about.

(Beat.)

You know… if your mother is still alive, things would be much easier. She always wanted you to be the chemist. You probably don't remember.

EDDIE: It was four years ago.

HENRY: Her ancestors serve the Emperor. Make the medicine for the Emperor. Maybe even poison him, no one is sure. Either way, require great skill!

(Beat.)

Since she has died, all you do is work. No time to study properly, no time even for a girlfriend. I blame you for not passing the A-level, but I know you cannot concentrate. Sometimes, I think: at least if you do not pass, you can run the business... take it over... But even then, where can it go? Have just enough to live, but can not afford to move, expand the business, or even take the holiday... You run the takeaway, will never be the millionaire. And every parent want his children to live better than him.

EDDIE: *(Pulls out the letter.)* Dad...

HENRY: And then, today... everything change! I get a very important phone call... It is from the local newspaper. The shop: they are going to do a story about it!

EDDIE: Story...?

HENRY: Yes, feature! A 'profile'! For the 'column'! Can you believe it?

EDDIE: Why would they...

HENRY: Why does any shop have the article about them in the paper! Because we are the 'noteworthy business', the 'success story'! People come in, pass by outside, appreciate the hard work, tell all their friend! Ey, my boy – your old man, he is a success!

EDDIE: Congratulations!

HENRY: Is the congratulations for us both! For the whole family, ah? Don't you see: now, there is the 'good backup' if you don't pass the A-level. You do not become the chemist, you take over the successful business! Success gives you the *choice*, you see?

(EDDIE notices for the first time two empty glasses on the counter, with an open bottle of sparkling grape juice. HENRY continues as he fills the glasses and hands one to EDDIE.)

First install the new telly; next, maybe, expand the shop – who knows! Or open the second shop on Oxford Street, what do you think? Can you imagine. Your mother, she would say, 'Must be a mistake!'

EDDIE: *(Beat; barely hiding his disappointment.)* It's brilliant, Dad... Really brilliant...

HENRY: Mmm! Is because of the whole family effort. I don't always say how much I appreciate you work hard. Is not part of our culture, you know.

#4   **Me and My Son**   (Henry)

But now, everything different, ah?
(Sung.)
Me and my son,
Running the shop,
Building the business,
Aim for the top,
Me and my son,
Everyone stop,
Say, 'Here is the highest quality.'
Me and my son,
Swapping the thought,
Sharing the secret,
Just as they ought.
Me and my son,
Battles are fought,
But only the highest quality!
People, they say we have different mind;
People, they are not wrong.
But people forget when the family is strong,
No one stays angry too long.
Me and my son,
Smart as they come,
Make the good memory,
Honour his mum.
Father and son,
When they are chum,
There is no higher quality.
It is the highest quality.
(Spoken.)
Ey, you know what? They are sending the photographer on Saturday.
I tell them, has to be a picture of the whole family!

EDDIE: Whole family?

HENRY: You and me! Will be nice to have the good picture of the two of
us together, ah? Before you move out, run the shop in Oxford Street!
Ey, you can help me write down the history of the business so we can
give it to him, fix my English!

EDDIE: Dad…

HENRY: Ah?

EDDIE: My results came.

HENRY: Ah?

(Beat. The moment of truth…)

EDDIE: I passed.

HENRY: You –

EDDIE: I passed!

(Beat.)

HENRY: *(Patting EDDIE on the back awkwardly. He should be happy…)*
My boy, my boy… See what the hard work will do? I know he can do it!

(Re: the letter, putting two and two together.)

Ey, is that the scores…?

(Reaches for it.)

EDDIE: *(Putting it back in his pocket.)* No, no, I put them upstairs.

HENRY: Aw. Safer there, will not get lost.

(Beat; self-disparaging.)

'Second shop in Oxford Street'! What does the university student need with that, ah? Small potato.

(Awkwardly putting his arm around EDDIE.)

Now the picture will be the farewell too, ah? Put it in the frame, hang it behind the counter, next to the picture of your mother. Every time I look at it, think about my successful son at the university, our time together… Can you imagine?

EDDIE: Yeah.

HENRY: Father, son, mother: happy family.

(With a tinge of sadness.)

Happy family…
(Sung.)
Parent and child, they are so much the same,
Never can know their own…
And when one is ready, the other is grown –
Parent is left all alone.
Me and my son,
Taking the cake.
Toasting the future,
Getting the break.
Me and my son,
Made the mistake…
From here on, the highest quality.
Only the highest quality.
Here:

(Toasts.)

To the highest quality.

(The two stand, sipping from the glasses in silence, watching the flickering images dance across the twin screens.)

SCENE FIVE

(EDDIE steps towards the audience as lights fade on HENRY and the takeaway.)

EDDIE: 'I passed.' 'I passed'?! What am I, a lemming? Honestly, though, can you blame me, facing an eternity of –

(Looking around.)

this? 'Second shop on Oxford Street'… That's the problem with us. Small eyes, smaller dreams. Do you know the great Chinese contribution to the modern world? I mean, after the takeaway? Gunpowder. Trouble is, we never got 'round to inventing a gun. I mean, what good's being practical when you're always a step behind?

#5   **Chinaman's Chance**   (**Eddie, Lum**)

(LUM shuffles on in EDDIE's imagination as Exhibit A: 'a typical Chinese'.)

Poor John Chinaman,
Ching chong Chinaman…
Dream as he might he just can't get ahead.

LUM: *(Very thick accent – 'success-fo', etc..)*
I try for successful
and end up the messful!

EDDIE: A sad, wan Chinaman
Is John Chinaman.
Hanging his hopes but on yesterday's thread…

LUM: I tell you, is all very stressful!

(Trying to sell his wares.)

Laundry and food
And back-rub include…
Come see!
for free – !
Fake DVD
And stolen TV –

EDDIE: Come try!
No buy?
Poor he!

LUM: *(Overlapping, furiously railing at an imaginary customer.)* Ni zhe ge xiao qi gui! Qu ni ma de!

EDDIE: Poor John Chinaman…

LUM: Ni bu yao lian de dongxi!

EDDIE: Scheme on, Chinaman…!

LUM: Wo pei!

EDDIE: Here you will stay 'til the day that you're dead,
It's what you might call, well…

LUM: Depressful!

EDDIE, LUM: Chinaman!
  Ding-dong-y,
  Ching-chong-y
  Chinaman – !
  Whoa-whoa-whoa-whoa-whoa!

  (LUM exits.)

#6   Who is to Blame?   (Angela, Reese, Dillon, Sheila, Lum)

EDDIE: So now what? Would be so much easier if I didn't care. If I were
  Reese Parker-Bennett, it would be 'Sorry, Dad. Not for me. Laters!'
  But the awful thing? I'm twenty-one, trapped, fighting for my very
  existence – pardon the hyperbole – and I actually care. Ain't parents
  a bitch?

  *(One by one, lights come up on DILLON, ANGELA, REESE, SHEILA and LUM as
  EDDIE watches as they deal with their respective parents that night.)*

DILLON: *(To her mother.)* Aw, I told you not to wait up… I was out with
  Eddie, it's his birthday… Eddie… yeah, well, why did you give me
  the card then? …

  (Sulking.)

  No… No, he wasn't…! God!

  (Under her breath.)

  He doesn't even *know* Delroy…!

ANGELA: *(Sung.)* What should I tell her?

REESE: Why do I bother?

DILLON: How do they always know?

SHEILA: Why do I repel her?

REESE: I am not my father.

DILLON: When will they let go?
  There goes another gem…

REESE, SHEILA, ANGELA, DILLON: How could we come from them…
  Are we just the same?

ANGELA: Oh… who is to blame…?

SHEILA: *(On the phone.)* I told you, Mum, I'm already seeing someone…
  Why do you have to be so intrusive… 'intrusive: meddlesome,
  interfering'! You're a bloody busybody! You wouldn't understand. No,
  you wouldn't.

REESE: *(On the phone.)* Mum! Did you get my message about Saturday
  night? …Yeah, you don't have to use 'em, I get them for free! I just
  put you on the list… Right.

(Disappointed.)

No no no, I understand.

(Chipper.)

Next time?

ANGELA: *(On the phone, leaving a hurried voicemail.)* Hullo, sorry I haven't called, you're probably asleep! Really busy at work, so much to do –

(Beat; annoyed.)

Oh, you're up… No, it's alright.

(It's torture.)

Put him on…

DILLON: If I were brighter…

ANGELA: If I were dumber…

REESE: If I could catch that ball…

DILLON: If I were a writer…

SHEILA: If I were a plumber…

REESE, SHEILA, ANGELA, DILLON: Would things change at all?

DILLON: When do I call their bluff?

ALL: When will I be enough?
  It's all such a game.

SHEILA: Oh… who is to blame…?

ALL: Good night,
  Sleep tight.
  Maybe when I wake,
  I'll be
  More like –

REESE: – What you planned to make.

LUM: *(On the phone, on automatic pilot.)* Mm. Mm. Mm. Mm. Mm.

(Beat.)

Mm.

(Longer beat.)

Mm.

(Beat; exasperated.)

Aiya, Ma…! Ni bie ku le!

SHEILA: When do I see her?

REESE: What do I bring her?

DILLON: How will I slip away?

ANGELA: If I were to be her –

SHEILA: If I only ring her –

DILLON, SHEILA, ANGELA: – Would it be okay?

REESE, SHEILA, ANGELA, DILLON: Why don't I try and move?
    What have I got to prove?
    Or am I just lame?

DILLON: Oh… Who is to blame…?

ANGELA: What should I tell her?

REESE: Why do I bother?

DILLON: How do they always know?

SHEILA: Why do I repel her?

REESE: I am not my father.

ANGELA,
DILLON: When will they let go?

ALL: And if I've never cared,
    Why do I get so scared?
    It's really a shame…
    Oh… who is to blame…?

ANGELA: What should I tell her?

SHEILA: Do I repel her?

REESE: Why do I bother?
    I'm not my father.

DILLON: If I were brighter…

ANGELA: If I were dumber…

LUM: Oh… who is to blame…?

DILLON: If I were brighter…

ANGELA: If I were dumber…

REESE: If I could catch that ball…

DILLON: If I were a writer…

SHEILA: If I were a plumber…

REESE,
SHEILA: Would things change at all?

SCENE SIX

(Lights change. The set changes as music shifts.

The next morning. Music as HENRY is out and about in the city.

He visits a newsstand in the Tube station…)

HENRY: *(To CASHIER.)* Which is the English language newspaper?

CASHIER: *(Taken aback.)* What, you mean the newspapers in English?
    (Gesturing everywhere.)
    Well… er… all over. Which one are you looking for?

HENRY: *(Overwhelmed by the selection)* Woh…! Mmm… one of each!

CASHIER: Come again – ?

HENRY: *(Impatient.)* One of each! I take one of each!

    (Music brings HENRY, his arms now full of newspapers, to a marketplace in Chinatown, where he is purchasing a few tins of tea and teacakes…)

CHINESE GROCER: *(To HENRY.)* Wah, so many newspaper! What happen, your son get arrested?

HENRY: Is the research. You know, since they are doing the story on my shop.

CHINESE GROCER: Yi? I did not hear!

HENRY: *(Nonchalant.)* Aw, ya, ya… You know, the business profile. Talk about the history… interview… nice picture of me and my son! Oh, and did I tell you he is going to the Oxford?

CHINESE GROCER: Wuah! Success in the business *and* the life! I will tell all my friends, look out for the big man!

(More music brings HENRY to the lobby of a small tower block, carrying the newspapers, tea and teacakes. A DOORMAN accosts him.)

DOORMAN: Here now, we don't want any!

HENRY: No, please, I am here to see Widow Chu?

DOORMAN: Widow Chu?

(Looking closely at him.)

Oh, it's you… Go on up.

(HENRY ascends the steps and we have finally arrived at…

The flat of the stately WIDOW CHU in Kensington.

The place reeks of long-faded glamour: ornate curtains, dated publicity photos in gold frames, the occasional piece of expensive Chinese furniture or mid-1980s objet d'art, everything immaculate yet somehow seeming covered in a faint layer of dust. The walls are in bad need of painting.

HENRY is pouring tea for WIDOW CHU. The tea cakes have been laid out on a chipped, ornate plate.

Although WIDOW CHU speaks with a Cantonese accent, her manner is much more refined than any of the Chinese we have met so far.)

WIDOW CHU: Newspaper, you say? Which one?

HENRY: *(Showing her his stack of newspapers.)* Well, it is not clear. I will confirm when they come for the picture on Saturday.

WIDOW CHU: And the Oxford… is very prestigious. Is the double celebration.

HENRY: I hope you will… ah… honour us with your company then. I'm sure they will be very excited to meet the famous Hong Kong movie star!

WIDOW CHU: Aiya, it has been many many years… That life, it is a distant memory. Show business – I do not even think about it anymore.

HENRY: Once a movie star, always a movie star. Is in your – how do you say – 'carriage'.

WIDOW CHU: You are not wrong.

(With just a hint of bitterness.)

The young actors nowadays, all they do is look this way, look that way, say the line. But they do not have the 'star quality'.

HENRY: Just so.

WIDOW CHU: Is like Cliff Richard once told me, 'Some people have it and some people don't, and baby, you have it'.

HENRY: Wuah…

WIDOW CHU: Also, Stevie Wonder.

(Beat.)

You must find out who is this newspaper. I know these – ah – 'media type'. They cannot be trusted. If it is the '*London Time* ', I will not be there. Always find a reason to give me the bad review.

HENRY: Mmm. The Westerner, they can be so disrespectful. And they have different taste.

WIDOW CHU: Is okay, look at their food. Heavy and always deep-fry. Have no appreciation for subtlety. Especially with Chinese food. I go to the Chinese restaurant here and I am frightened. In Hong Kong we have delicate sauce, ah? Here it is gravy.

HENRY: Not all Chinese restaurant here, ah?

WIDOW CHU: No, of course not… I am speaking of a particular kind that caters to Western taste. The kind that serve chips.

(Beat. HENRY shifts uncomfortably.)

Most people have this problem: like only what they are familiar with. Only eat one kind of food, listen to one kind of music, speak one kind of language.

HENRY: Not like you…!

WIDOW CHU: Even when I am young, I know the world is getting smaller!

HENRY: You are ahead of your time…

WIDOW CHU: This 'globalisation': to me, it is the old hat. In Hong Kong, most of the singers perform only the Cantonese songs. Maybe Mandarin. Me, I sing the English songs, the French songs, the German songs… Hebrew songs… I am the first Hong Kong singer to perform the jazz, the Jacques Brel, the reggae… all on the same record! Make an entire movie in Mexican…

HENRY: Hwah! They do not appreciate you here. Is the waste of the world-class talent!

WIDOW CHU: *(Just the slightest bit offended.)* Is not all that bad…! My husband, Mr Chu, before he died, told me it is a mistake to stay in Hong Kong when the Communists take over. Then, he died. I sell everything, buy a first-class ticket, flat in Kensington. Now everything in Hong Kong is the same, China is rich, Joan Chen is directing movies...

(This last detail is clearly distasteful to her.)

But I am happy I am here. You know why? Because no matter how much money is in China, underneath it is still the 'peasant mentality'. You cannot buy the 'class'. London, it has the 'class', the 'star quality'.

HENRY: You cannot have the 'class' without the hard work, ah?

WIDOW CHU: And *time*. You must be born with class, one generation cannot learn it.

HENRY: I know, I know. I come to London a poor man, but my family, it is descended from the Imperial Court...!

WIDOW CHU: Really?

HENRY: Mmm!

WIDOW CHU: I sense this...! I do not know it, but I sense it! Otherwise, we would have nothing in common! My husband, Mr. Chu, before he died, liked to say, 'Two peas in a pod, even when they are shelled, can still fit them together!'

HENRY: You know, Widow Chu, my wife and I, we make this long trip together, start the business from nothing, raise a son... After she died, I think, 'Why do I want to find anyone else? She is the – you know – love of my life.' And I have the son to support, there is no time to look anyway.

WIDOW CHU: Is very romantic.

HENRY: I want to preserve the memory. But lately I am thinking, especially with my son going to the Oxford and the business success... Perhaps it is time to look after myself, ah?

(Pregnant pause.)

For a year and a half, up until yesterday, I am content to be only the fan who is lucky enough to be in the tea house when you forget your purse...

WIDOW CHU: So embarrass...

HENRY: Today, I want to – ah – present myself to you... the owner of a successful business with the promising future, hoping maybe you are feeling the same way...?

(Slight beat.)

Do not answer, do not answer! Come to tea Saturday, ah? See the shop, meet my son. Then make the decision.

WIDOW CHU: Mmm.

(A moment. Then, thoughtfully:)

One must not – as my husband, Mr. Chu, liked to say... before he died – 'dig the grave for the dog when the master has expired', ah?

(Beat.)

I think I will wear the green dress. Joan Chen, she cannot wear green…!

SCENE SEVEN

(Later that day, at the takeaway.

EDDIE sits at the counter. DILLON stands in front of him with her bike.)

DILLON: You told him *what*?! Have you completely lost it?

EDDIE: No, I've got it all sorted out. Found this site, 'quality-fake-degrees-dot-com'? You can buy a quality-fake-A-level certificate for 160 US. It's not like Dad knows what they really look like anyway!

DILLON: Then what? It's not going to get you into a university!

EDDIE: One step at a time. Figured we could go in on it together… For 180 you can also get a quality-fake-marriage-license!

DILLON: Oh, well, that's a – where am I going to get 90 dollars!

EDDIE: Doesn't Panni work in finance? Or Delroy!

DILLON: What kind of girl do you think I am?!

(EDDIE'S mobile rings.)

God, there it goes again! Who's calling you, you don't have any friends!

EDDIE: *(Nervous.)* Damned telemarketers…

(We hear a voicemail beep and SHEILA appears at the side of the stage, on the phone.)

SHEILA: Hello, my foreign Prince… have you thought about my Racial Encounter Group on Friday…? I haven't heard from you since yesterday. I read about a Chinese herb that could help us with your problem…? Please, Eddie…

(Very emotional.)

Wo xiang nian ni zhe me duo, wo xiang zi sha le!

(Disappears.)

DILLON: You know who could help out?

EDDIE: I don't want to talk about him!

DILLON: He's a really good guy, and so beautiful! Give him a chance…!

(EDDIE's mobile rings again.)

Will you just answer it!

(Voicemail beep. ANGELA appears with a cat o' nine tails.)

ANGELA: Hello, my Yellow Warrior! Have you thought about my Rally for the Victims of the 2004 Morecambe Bay Cockling Disaster? It might be just what we need to get over your – ah – problem? I hope you aren't trying to avoid me. I would have to punish you…!

(Cracks the whip as she disappears.)

EDDIE: You just be careful. Don't let's forget what he is, eh?

DILLON: You mean gorgeous?

EDDIE: I mean a narcissist!

DILLON: Oh, Eddie…!

EDDIE: They charm you 'til they've got you, then the rush is over and it's off to the next conquest.

DILLON: Are you jealous, Eddie?

(EDDIE's mobile rings again. SHEILA appears at the side of the stage.)

Oh – !

(Grabs the mobile from EDDIE and answers it.)

He doesn't want any!

(Hangs up on a shocked SHEILA.

LUM enters from the kitchen with a takeaway carton.)

LUM: *(Flinging the takeaway carton on the counter, disgusted.)* 'Chips'!
(Exits.)

DILLON: *(Picking up the order and getting on her bike; to herself.)* Hmmm!

EDDIE: What?

DILLON: Nothing… Just didn't know you cared!

(Exits.

Beat. EDDIE's mobile rings again. SHEILA appears in her spot, annoyed. Then we hear a call waiting beep. ANGELA appears in her spot, equally annoyed.)

EDDIE: Ahhh!

(He looks at his mobile and is about to answer it when REESE enters.)

REESE: Eddie!

(EDDIE silences his mobile abruptly. SHEILA and ANGELA disappear.)

EDDIE: *(To the audience.)* If there was a God, there are times I'd swear He's got it in for me.

REESE: All right?

EDDIE: Yeah…!

(Beat.)

Did you see Dillon?

REESE: *(Puzzled.)* No.

EDDIE: She wasn't here, actually.

REESE: Right.

EDDIE: It's not as if she works here or anything.

REESE: Right!

(Going up to the Laughing Buddha on the counter and rubbing its belly.)

Hey, I remember this!

(A note on the counter catches his eye. Reading.)

'Quality-fake-degrees-dot-com'.

EDDIE: Can I help you with something? I'm a little busy – !

REESE: Actually –

(Fishes around in his rucksack and produces a package which has been carefully but ineptly wrapped.)

Happy birthday.

(EDDIE is stunned.)

You left yesterday before I could give it to you.

(Beat.)

Well, open it!

(EDDIE does. It is a DVD.)

EDDIE: *(Smiling.) Charlie and the Chocolate Factory*!

REESE: I got it for you right before your mum died. Put off giving it to you and then, well… afterwards, it just didn't seem right. Remember, she wouldn't let you watch it 'cos Johnny Depp looked like –

REESE, EDDIE: – Michael Jackson!

EDDIE: I remember.

REESE: Always sort of envied that. I mean, that she cared. My mum and dad let me watch *Silence of the Lambs* when I was eleven.

EDDIE: Wow.

REESE: Well, they didn't find out, anyway. Kind of had their own lives, you know?

EDDIE: Couldn't get rid of mine.

REESE: It shows. I mean, in a good way.

(Beat.)

So are you together, then?

EDDIE: What, Dillon and me? No, can you imagine?

REESE: Never even shagged…? You must have snogged her once or twice!

(Beat.)

Well, *she* likes *you*.

EDDIE: Pffft!

REESE: Sure, you always know when they fight – !

EDDIE: You fancy her?

REESE: Not bad looking. Seeing her later… told her I'd help her practice.

EDDIE: She any good?

REESE: She's terrible!

EDDIE: Why encourage her, then!

REESE: She wants it so badly, shouldn't that be enough?

EDDIE: See, that's what people hate about you!

REESE: *(Genuinely hurt.)* People hate me?

EDDIE: 'Shouldn't that be enough'! Easy for you to say, being at the top of the bloody food chain! Yeah, sure – roll out of bed looking like that, the world opens its doors to you!

REESE: Nah. Really?

EDDIE: *(Annoyed.)* 'Really?' You ever shopped for clothes and not had your pick of the shop? Choose whatever you like, you'll look great! You're the bloody target demographic, aren't you!

(REESE throws a fortune cookie at him.)

Hey – !

REESE: *(Playful.)* You think too much!

EDDIE: *(Re: the fortune cookies.)* These cost money, you know!

REESE: I mean, what would be so bad if you got up there tomorrow night and did the same thing?

EDDIE: *Britain's Newest Unexpected Singing Sensation*? Not bloody likely!

REESE: Why not!

EDDIE: *(At his wits' end.)* Well, look at me…!

REESE: *(Shrugs.)* I'd do you.

(Beat.)

Why are you so hard on yourself? You seeing anyone? Got a girlfriend?

EDDIE: No.

REESE: Shame. I could introduce you – oh, you *do* like –

EDDIE: *(Offended.)* Yes, of course! God – !

REESE: Just asking! Wouldn't matter if you *were*…

(EDDIE's mobile rings. He answers the takeaway phone instead.)

EDDIE: Hello, Happy Family…! Hello?

(Realises his mistake and hangs up.)

REESE: *(As EDDIE silences his mobile.)* Think about what I said. No man is an island.

(Beginning to leave.)

'Before love, I was no one. Now, I am *so* one.'

(Beat.)

Don't think I care for that one…

(And one more thing….)

Oh, and 'quality-fake-degrees-dot-com'? Totally overpriced.

(Exits.

EDDIE's mobile starts ringing once more.)

#7   **Before Love**   **(Sheila, Angela, Dillon)**

EDDIE: *(To the mobile.)* Ugh! Leave me alone!

(To the audience.)

'Love'! My generation? We're all bloody obsessed with it! It's like a sickness. Tom's generation? Now they had their priorities straight. It was only three years ago Tom wrote his first love song to his wife, and they've been married over fifty years! Today you're lucky if a person don't burst into song after fifty *seconds…*

(SHEILA enters in EDDIE's fantasy and begins to stalk him about the stage, desperate to explain her feelings for him.)

SHEILA: Before love, there was nothing
But the sound of an echo
As I woke in the morning
With my lips on my pillow.
Before love, I was empty.
I was void. I was formless.
I would look in the mirror
And be sick in the basin.
Before love, you'd annoy me
If you asked how was my day.
Before love, it would destroy me
If I walked in the room and I heard Marvin Gaye.
Before love, I was no one.
Now with love, girl, I am *so* one!
Before love, unending drama –
Now I talk nice to my mama…!
Before love, I'd pass through ya.
Now with love, now I say, 'Booyah!'
For there ain't no 'Hallelujah'
'Til you're someone –
Someone –

Any kinda sorta someone
Who loves!
Oooh…

(EDDIE is backed into a corner. Suddenly, ANGELA emerges behind him and begins to stalk him as well.)

ANGELA: Before love, I would grovel
In my own private puddle
With a gut full of pity
And a jug of Ribena.

(As if that weren't enough, DILLON emerges and joins the fray.)

DILLON: Before love, I was loveless
And my sex life meant nothing.
Now I see you in visions
When I sleep… with my boyfriend!

SHEILA: Before love, I was surly
As I'd ask, on without end…

ANGELA: Why are Chinese men so girly?

DILLON: And should nice girls be thinking of doing their friend…?

SHEILA, ANGELA, DILLON: Before love, we had no one.
Before love, life would, well, blow one.
Now with love, gone is the darkness –

ANGELA: When I pass, dogs seem to bark less…!

SHEILA, ANGELA, DILLON: Before love, zero meaning.
Now with love, Mint Listerining.
'Cos there ain't no point in cleaning
Without someone –
Someone –
Someone kinda sorta maybe someone –

(REESE enters and EDDIE is suddenly plunged into memory. He and REESE are 15, isolated in their own light.)

REESE: Come on, then! I'll buy the popcorn.

EDDIE: I can't! My mum – !

REESE: She's not gonna find out!

EDDIE: You don't know her, she's everywhere. Like the Oracle, man.

REESE: The Oracle?

EDDIE: You know, from *The Matrix*.

REESE: Anorak!

EDDIE: Am not!

REESE: 'Like the Oracle, man'… Putting 'man' at the end don't make you any more cool, you know!

EDDIE: Stop…

REESE: Come on, you can be like, my date!

EDDIE: Get out!

REESE: *(Play-acting.)* Come on, beautiful…!

    (And suddenly we're not quite sure…)

EDDIE: *(Uncomfortable but tempted.)* No…

REESE: *(Looking him in the eye; beat.)* So?

    (REESE leans over and kisses him. REESE disappears as EDDIE returns to the present, completely gobsmacked by the memory.)

SHEILA, ANGELA, DILLON: *(Welcoming a humiliated EDDIE into their fold.)* Before love, life was worthless!
Before love, God, were we mirthless!
Before love, what did it matter?
We were lost and so much fatter!

Before love, frozen chicken;
Now with love: pulses, they quicken
'Cos you know, life's finger-lickin'
When there's someone –
Someone –
Someone who is kinda sorta maybe someone –

    (EDDIE turns to the audience and whimpers.)

SHEILA: – you love!

SHEILA, ANGELA, DILLON: Love!
Love!
Love!
Love…!

    (Blackout.)

SCENE EIGHT

(The following night: karaoke at The Flying Nanny.

An OFF-PITCH R&B SINGER is finishing her song on a makeshift stage – and very much living up to her name – as the scene opens.

The room is full of hopeful CONTESTANTS. EDDIE stands as DILLON flips through a binder containing a list of songs. The song ends to thunderous indifference.

The SINGER passes EDDIE.)

EDDIE: Good job…

(She scowls at him and exits.)

DILLON: Don't talk to the other contestants, you'll only encourage them!

(Calling after her.)

You were shite!

EDDIE: Jeez!

DILLON: It's just showbiz, Eddie. She won't take it personally. Now why aren't you talking? You're supposed to be pumping up my alter-ego!

EDDIE: Shut up, I'm here, aren't I?!

DILLON: Well, focus!

(Continuing to flip through the binder.)

Where the hell is 'Slut Goddess'? What kind of place is this?

EDDIE: *(Glancing over her shoulder at the binder, excited.)*

Ooh, 'Help Yourself'. That's a good one.

(Pointing at another.)

'Daughter of Darkness'!

(And another.)

'Lusty Lady'!

(As if he's doing a 'Word Search' puzzle.)

'Dr. Love'!

(Half-singing to himself, in the stratosphere.)

'Puppet Man…!'

(DILLON snaps the binder shut, having had enough.)

DILLON: Number 326. I found it. I mean, who's ever heard of these songs?

EDDIE: They're good.

DILLON: How would you know? Who sang them – ?

EDDIE: *(Hesitant.)* Tom Jones.

DILLON: Tom Jones?! No one our age listens to Tom Jones!

EDDIE: *(Embarrassed.)* He's a national treasure.

DILLON: *Tom Jones*?! 'Sex Bomb' Tom Jones? What, do you fancy him?

EDDIE: No!

DILLON: Right!

EDDIE: I don't bloody well fancy Tom Jones!

DILLON: Don't you? Do you know anything that's *not* Tom Jones?

EDDIE: *(Pointing at the binder – the last song he'd spotted.)* 'Sing Your Song'.

DILLON: My what?

EDDIE: No, it's the title. It's a Remy Hoffer song.

(DILLON gives him a look. Guilty.)

They did it together in a concert once…

(REESE enters.)

REESE: Hullo!

DILLON: Reese!

REESE: Nervous?

DILLON: *(Playing cool.)* No, easy-peasy! Some of these people are really talented… that last one?

REESE: *(To EDDIE.)* You alright? Think about what I said?

(Gives EDDIE a wink.)

EDDIE: *(Under his breath.)* God – !

REESE: *(To both.)* I'll be back there, if you need anything. Break a leg!

(Exits.)

DILLON: *(Love struck.)* Alas, Panroy. I knew you well.

EDDIE: Panni.

DILLON: *(In a daze.)* Him, too.

(Lowering her eyes, speaking to the air.)

What? Oh, yes, my little darling…

(Shifting her eyes.)

Aren't you sweet…

(And once more.)

Mummy loves *you* very much, too…

(To EDDIE.)

Look, Eddie: it's all our beautiful unborn children…!

CONTEST STAFF MEMBER: *(Over the sound system.)* Number 38, Dillon Diwan.

DILLON: *(To EDDIE, indicating the imaginary CHILDREN.)* Watch them for me, will you?

(DILLON scrambles to the stage. A spotlight hits her and suddenly she is a deer caught in headlights. Nervously.)

Er… Number 3… 326…

EDDIE: Breathe!

(The music for 'Slut Goddess' begins. It plays. And plays. DILLON stands there, petrified. She opens her mouth and a few pitiful squeaks come out, then it's all over.)

CONTEST STAFF MEMBER: *(Over the sound system.)* Thank you!

DILLON: *(Snapping out of it; hysterical.)* No… wait! I'm ready now, I can do it! Start the music!

CONTEST STAFF MEMBER: *(Over the sound system.)* I'm sorry, Miss. Only one chance per act.

DILLON: *(Re: the DJ.)* No, he started it too early, I never said I was ready – !

(The other CONTESTANTS begin to grumble.)

EDDIE: *(Moving towards the stage to help her off.)* Come on, Dill…

CONTEST STAFF MEMBER: *(Over the sound system.)* Sorry, Miss… we've got to be fair to everyone…

DILLON: Wait!

(Reaches out and pulls EDDIE onto the stage.)

CONTEST STAFF MEMBER: *(Over the sound system.)* You've already had your turn, Miss… One chance per act.

DILLON: I'm with him!

EDDIE: What?

DILLON: We're a duo. That counts as a new act, don't it? You never said we couldn't enter in more than one category!

CONTEST STAFF MEMBER: *(Over the sound system, weary.)* Please, Miss…

DILLON: Reese!

CONTEST STAFF MEMBER: *(Over the sound system.)* Hold on…

(Beat.

We hear a faint VOICE FROM THE CROWD.)

VOICE FROM THE CROWD: *(Barely audible.)* Oi! Check it out! Jackie Chan over here gonna sing…!

EDDIE: *(To DILLON, whispering.)* Come on, Dill, let's just go.

DILLON: *(Whispering.)* I need you, Eddie. Just get me started and I'll be fine.

(Points at a monitor.)

The words are over there. We'll pick something you know.

EDDIE: I don't think this is a good idea –

CONTEST STAFF MEMBER: *(Over the sound system.)* Right, what are you going to sing?

DILLON: 'Sing Your Song'!

CONTEST STAFF MEMBER: My what?

DILLON: It's the title! 'Sing Your Song'!

CONTEST STAFF MEMBER: *(Over the sound system.)* Right.

(Beat, then, deliberately.)

Are you ready?

#8   Sing Your Song   **(Eddie, Company)**

(The music to 'Sing Your Song' begins. DILLON freezes once more. EDDIE looks to her, then to the audience, and suddenly we're out of space and time.)

EDDIE: *(To the audience.)* In some alternate reality, I might have been a physicist. There's something so comforting in the notion that everything in the universe has an explanation. I was always quite keen on Einstein's Theory of Relativity, which says that energy and mass are the same thing. 'Cos when you couple that with the law of conservation of energy, it means nothing is ever truly created or destroyed, just recycled.

(Beat.)

I wouldn't have discovered Tom Jones if Mum hadn't died. Father insisted on a Western-style service, but being strapped for cash and a devout atheist, we wound up at the discount church down at the end of High Street. The funeral went off without a hitch, until the very end, when Mum's casket was to be carried off for its journey to the crematorium. Somehow the CD for the Woo funeral had gotten mixed up with the CD for the Schmidt-Godowski wedding, and so she ended up making her final exit to the strains of 'Witch Queen of New Orleans'. There, in my moment of greatest need, the Voice found me, proof that somehow, in some crazy way, we're all made from the same stuff: Mum, Dad, the Schmidt-Godowskis, Tom Jones and me.

(EDDIE closes his eyes and tries to hear the music in his head.

Freely, finding his legs.)

When all the world has come undone
And there is nowhere left to run,
Just close your eyes and sing a song,
Sing a song, sing your song…
'Cos when the music's clear and bright,
There's not a thing that can't go right,
So make it strong and bring the light,
Sing your song…
Sing your song and glory be,
All your cares are out at sea.
What was sad is something tragic and sublime.
Sing your song and all your woes
Go the way of Navajos
When they're sung in sixteen bars and quarter-time!
Oh…

(Finding the tempo.)

So when your life is cold and grey
And nothing ever goes your way,
You sing your song, and with your song, you can belong…
So hear my song: sing my song, sing your song!

(Spots up on HENRY, SHEILA, ANGELA, REESE and LUM as they appear in EDDIE's delighted imagination and sing with him, encouraging and validating him in a way they never have in real life. It is a moment of delirious joy and pure fantasy: silly, cheesy and heartbreakingly sad.)

COMPANY: When life is strictly under par,
And no one sees the man you are,
Just close your eyes and sing your song,
Sing your song, sing your song.
When you're the man the fates forsake,
The one who cannot catch a break,
Anesthetise and sing your song,
Sing your song,
Sing the moon and sing the stars,
Sing of love to French guitars,
Sing a life and you can brace for any fall.
Sing a song and build your wall.
Sing as big as you feel small.
Be the man who finally gets to have it all.
When all the world is closing in,
When love's a game you just can't win,
Just sing your song and make it strong and you'll belong…
Just sing your song…

EDDIE: Sing my song…

COMPANY: Sing your song…

EDDIE: Sing my song…

COMPANY: Sing your song…

EDDIE: Sing my song…

COMPANY: Sing your song…

EDDIE: Sing my song…

COMPANY: *(Disappearing.)* Just sing your song,
Sing your song…

(And EDDIE is left alone, back onstage at The Flying Nanny.)

EDDIE: *(Riffing wildly like Tom Jones.)* Sing your song!

(Blackout.

Immediate segue to:)

SCENE NINE

(Outside The Flying Nanny, immediately following.

EDDIE, DILLON and REESE exit out onto the street. They are on Cloud Nine.
EDDIE has a piece of paper in his hand.)

DILLON: *(To EDDIE.)* Man, you smashed it! Did you see the geezer in the rugby shirt? Jaw was on the floor!

REESE: You should have heard the judges in back, asking where are all the other Chinese boys!

EDDIE: *(Embarrassed.)* Stop! …

(Mopping the sweat from his brow.)

I'm drenched!

(To DILLON, apologetic.)

Didn't leave you much room to sing.

DILLON: You're out of my league, love. Might even go and Spotify me some Tom Jones when I get home!

REESE: Tom Jones…?

(Studying EDDIE for a moment.)

I can see it…!

DILLON: *(To REESE, indicating EDDIE.)* You want your '*Britain's Newest Unexpected Singing Sensation*'…!

(EDDIE laughs.)

I'm serious!

(To REESE.)

Look at him! What could be more unexpected than that?

#9   The New Chinese Tom Jones   (Dillon, Eddie, Reese, Company)

Who's that givin' 'em a massive shock?
Who's that makin' all of Britain rock?
Who's that throwin' off his father's wok?
It's the new Chinese Tom Jones!
Who's that tearin' up the British charts?
Who's that breakin' sixty million hearts?
Who's that grabbin' all his private parts?
It's the new Chinese Tom Jones!
Every little note he utters leaves 'em hazy.
Every little step he dances drips with sex.
Never have they gone so abso-flippin' crazy,
Lookin' at a skinny Chinese boy in specs!
Everybody loves a Cinderella story.
Everybody loves an underdog, it's true.

People really love it when a loser gets to shove it
And there's no one ever shoved quite as much as you!
Who's that spendin' like a bloody toff?
Who's that hangin' with the Hasselhoff?
Who's that tellin' 'em to all sod off
In the richest, dulcet tones?
The uncompromising,
Most surprising,
Star-who's-rising,
Galvanising,
Super-manly
New Chinese Tom Jones!

EDDIE: There is such a thing as too unexpected! Besides, final round's Saturday. I don't even know if I can make it.

(To DILLON.)

I really only did it for you.

DILLON: Have you gone mental?

EDDIE: It's only two days from now! And can you see my father giving me the night off so his only son can make a fool of himself on national telly?

DILLON: You'll talk to him. Reese'll talk to him! Department of Health will mysteriously shut the place down for the night. We'll find a way!
(Sung.)
Who's that bustin' out of his cocoon?
Who's that callin' out his own damn tune?
Who's that sleepin' 'til the crack of noon?
It's the new Chinese Tom Jones!
Who's that fella who is always seen?
Chuffed and chummy with the bloody Queen?
Who's that gettin' out of E-fifteen?
It's the new Chinese Tom Jones!
Never will he spend another dawn-to-midnight
Smothered in the scent of garlic, prawns and oil.
Never spend another 'no-one-ordered-squid'-night,
Finishing the lot before it starts to spoil.
Say goodbye to corny crank calls every morning…
Hold the 'number two' and 'number sixty-nine'.
Not another hour pushin' bloody sweet and sour,
I say, 'Hello, Happy Family', time to cut the line!

(She looks at EDDIE expectantly.)

EDDIE: Yeah… I really hate squid!
(Sung.)
Who's that riding in a black sedan?
Who's that sporting a December tan?

DILLON: Who's that visiting a dying fan?

EDDIE, DILLON: It's the new Chinese Tom Jones!

EDDIE: Who's that living offa wine and cheese?

DILLON: Who's that slumming in the Hebrides?

EDDIE: Who's that saving all the manatees?

EDDIE, DILLON: It's the new Chinese Tom Jones!
Nothing that he asks is ever any bother.
Anything he wants to do, the world says, 'yes'.

DILLON: Every other year, he goes to see his father
When they feel his nerves can handle all the stress.

EDDIE: All the little boys in Holland just adore him.

DILLON: So do all the toothless grannies in Beijing.

EDDIE: In the Chafarinas there's a tribe of Filipinas
Come to ask him if he'll be their honorary king!
Who's that louder than a thunderclap?

DILLON: Who's that closin' up the racial gap?

EDDIE: Who's so nasty he deserves a slap
For those freakish pheromones?

DILLON: He's the awe-inspiring,

EDDIE: Pistol-firing,

DILLON: Bra-acquiring,

EDDIE: Shy, retiring,

EDDIE, DILLON: Pelvis-pumpin'
New Chinese Tom Jones!

REESE: *(To DILLON, playing Devil's Advocate.)* Wait – now wait –
Let's all be realistic.
They may not get his style.
He's mad, he's great,
And even quite artistic
But there's really no predicting
If it's really worth his while.

(To EDDIE.)

Your father will disown you
And the audience may stone you…
Is that a kind of torture
That you're willing to endure?
(Beat. Then, deliberately.)
Who's that livin' on the outer fringe?
Who's that goin' on a booty binge?
Who's that makin' all the old folks cringe?
It's the new Chinese Tom Jones!

DILLON: Who's that rollin' for the new Rolls Royce?

REESE: Who's that singin' in his outdoor voice?

EDDIE: Who's that singin' 'cos he has a choice?

EDDIE, DILLON, REESE: It's the new Chinese Tom Jones!

EDDIE: Everybody has a chance to grab the glory,
   Everybody has a chance and then no more.
   Any more delaying and it's, 'Thanks a lot for playing',
   Baby, polish up my pants and let me hit the floor!

(The COMPANY appears in EDDIE's imagination, bringing the number to a big finish.)

EDDIE, DILLON, REESE, COMPANY: Who's that makin' all the ladies howl?
   Who's that bringin' back the 'tiger growl'?
   Who's just like him but without the jowl?
   It's the new Chinese Tom Jones!
   Who's that lookin' like he's underage?
   Who's that busted up the macho gauge?
   Who's that takin' up the whole damn stage?
   It's the new Chinese Tom Jones!
   Who's that lightin' up the Sixties flame?
   Big black white man in a Chinese frame?
   Who might worry if he had some shame?
   It's the new Chinese Tom Jones!
   It's the new Chinese Tom Jones!
   It's the new Chinese Tom Jones!
   It's the awe-inspiring,
   Shy, retiring,
   Galvanising,
   Most surprising,
   Super-manly
   New Chinese Tom Jones!

(The number ends. The COMPANY exits; underscore as the scene continues.)

DILLON: *(Checking her mobile and hopping on her bike.)* Uch, it's Mum. Look, you two bond. I've got to go.

   (To EDDIE.)

   Think about it is all I'm saying!

   (Mouths 'Call me later' to REESE.)

EDDIE: It's just, Dad – he'd die of shame. Then kill me. Then make me clean out the toilet for a month!

DILLON: *(Riding off.)* Have a little vision! What are you, a man or a mouth?

   (Exits.

   Beat.)

REESE: *(Getting close to EDDIE, reading the piece of paper in his hand.)*
Well, anyway, you've got your number and info about Saturday. Just remember to sign the release before you get there...

EDDIE: I will. Hey, Reese – thanks.

REESE: You were brilliant, really.

EDDIE: Yeah?

REESE: Yeah.

(Beat. They kiss, tentatively. It's not clear who makes the first move. Then, separate:)

EDDIE: Yeah?

REESE: Yeah!

(They really start to snog. Lights out.)

ACT TWO

PROLOGUE

#10   The Funeral   (Mourners, Lum, Angela, Sheila)

(The funeral of EDDIE's mother, in the discount church down at the end of High Street. It is winter. There is a casket upstage center. HENRY and EDDIE sit facing upstage, with a group of MOURNERS.

They sing a solemn hymn.)

MOURNERS: Jesus loves the alder and the shrub.
  Humble is his measure, fair is He.
  Jesus loves the maggot and the grub
  And He loveth even me.
  He is the light guideth from above.
  He is the hand giveth me a shove.
  Jesus even loves Beelzebub
  And the shows on ITV.

(EDDIE looks around, disoriented. Somber organ music continues.)

EDDIE: Mum…?

MOURNER: Shhhh!

EDDIE: *(To HENRY.)* Where did all of these people come from…? Mum didn't have any friends!

MOURNER: Eddie!

  (She turns around. It is SHEILA.)

  Don't disturb the King…!

EDDIE: Sheila…! Do I know you yet…?

  (To himself.)

  I'm so confused…

MOURNERS: *(Winding it up.)* Jesus loves the faggot and the schlub
  And the heathen dead Chineeeeeeee…

  (A PASTOR enters and begins the service.)

PASTOR: We come together this morning to say farewell to Eva Fang-Hua Woo: friend, neighbor… pioneer.

EDDIE: 'Pioneer'?!

SHEILA: Shhhh!

PASTOR: Faithful daughter of Bing-Bing and Jia-Ping, beloved wife of Henry and disappointed mother of Edmond, –

  (EDDIE reacts.)

– many were the hours she would spend among friends, speculating under which of our fair bridges her no-talent son would huddle in his twilight years, and will he be resourceful enough to build a fire for warmth out of the greasy flea-ridden rags which will constitute the sum of his worldly possessions…

EDDIE: No, that's not true!

(Another MOURNER turns around to address him. It is LUM.)

LUM: Some respect for the dead, thank you!

EDDIE: Lum! You *do* speak English!

LUM: Shen me? Shen jing bing!

PASTOR: To begin, a few words from our brother Lum.

(LUM goes up to the podium with some index cards.

Suddenly, DILLON enters noisily with her bike and clumsily finds her seat.)

DILLON: Sorry, sorry!

LUM: *(Screaming at her.)* Ni zhe ge ren: you ben, you ben zhuo, you chou! Hen si ni!

(Settles down and reads his cards, to the tune of 'Chinaman's Chance'.)

LUM: Ching chong chingchingchong…
Ching chong chingchingchong…
Ching ching ching ching ching ching chong chong chong chong,
Chong chingchong
Chong chingchong
Chong ching chong…

MOURNERS: *(Solemnly.)*
Chong chingchong
Chong chingchong
Chong ching chong…

PASTOR: And now, an elegy composed especially for this occasion by Miss Angela Wong, entitled 'Yellow'.

(ANGELA is revealed in a traditional Chinese mourner's hat and sash of muslin. She carries a lighter, which she lights as she sings.)

EDDIE: Angela…?

ANGELA: Yellow, his mother,
Yellow, his father,
Yellow, their sorrow,
Yellow, this flame.
Yellow, her kindness
Yellow, our blindness.
Yellow, her illness.
Yellow, our shame.

(Indicating a bowl of fruit offerings at the foot of the casket.)

In traditional Chinese funerals, we present offerings of food to our beloved deceased, so they may not experience hunger on their long journey ahead…

(But DILLON has gotten up and is standing over the bowl, selecting an apple for herself.)

DILLON: Thank God, I'm *starved*!

(Sits.)

ANGELA: *(Annoyed.)* So, too, do we burn effigies of money and earthly luxuries so they might enjoy the same comforts they enjoyed in life…

SHEILA: *(A squeal of delighted interest.)* Oh!

(To no one in particular.)

Isn't that just so – !

ANGELA: And so I make the ultimate sacrifice and offer to the dearly departed the thing she most wanted in life but could not have. A child of whom she could be proud…

(About to light herself on fire.)

I am coming, Mother Woo! I am coming! *Je suis fini*!

(Another MOURNER turns around. It is WIDOW CHU.)

WIDOW CHU: *(To EDDIE, re: ANGELA's French.)* Wai, she has the gift!

EDDIE: *(To DILLON.)* Who is *she*?

(DILLON takes a deafening crunch out of her apple.)

ANGELA: Yellow's the colour of her no-count son
Making her wish that she had never had one.
Eddie, how you shame her!
Can you blame her for checking out?
Look what you've done – you're the one we could all do without!

EDDIE: No, it's not true! You didn't even know her, any of you!

(ANGELA tries to light herself, but her lighter goes out. She tries again. Nothing. In frustration, she reads the manufacturing stamp.)

ANGELA: *(Bitterly.)* 'Made in China'!

PASTOR: Finally, a song celebrating the love and devotion between our Henry and his beloved wife…

(SHEILA gets up and proceeds to the podium.)

SHEILA: Before love,
He was nothing.
He was void, he was formless.
He would wake in the morning
With his lips on his pillow.

(HENRY begins to sob noisily.)

DILLON: Awww…

EDDIE: *(Embarrassed.)* Dad…

SHEILA: *(Continuing under the above.)* Before love,
    He was empty
    In his own private puddle
    With a gut full of pity
    And a jug of Ribena.

(By this time, HENRY is completely overcome and blubbering quite loudly.)

EDDIE: Dad…!

(Under the following, HENRY, overcome, begins to stagger to the casket, to EDDIE's horror.)

SHEILA: *(Accompanied by the other MOURNERS, who have become a gospel choir.)*
    Before love,
    He was no one,
    Now with love,
    Now he is so one!
    'Cos with love,
    Gone is the darkness!
    In the sea, sharks seem to shark less!

(As SHEILA and the choir continue, HENRY flings the cover of the casket wide open and takes the body of his dead wife into his arms.)

EDDIE: No! Dad!

SHEILA: Before love,
    Nothing to ya.
    Now with love,
    People would do ya!
    'Cos we all 'Praise, Hallelujah!'
    When there's someone, someone,
    Any kind of sort of type of style of maybe someone –

(HENRY kisses the body on the lips. All of a sudden, the body turns to the audience and is revealed to be REESE.)

EDDIE: Noooooo!

(All hell breaks loose. Screams all around as a CHINESE LION with the head of Tom Jones rushes on and begins to chase the women around the stage, trying to swallow them each into its gaping maw.

The set behind them changes as we segue to the next scene.)

SCENE ONE

(Immediately following. Early morning. EDDIE wakes up in his room. He turns, notices REESE next to him, in bed, still asleep. EDDIE panics, slips out of bed, dresses hurriedly. REESE stirs.)

REESE: Mmmmrphhhh…

EDDIE: Shhh!

(Rushes out into the next room to make sure HENRY is not awake.

REESE sits up, rubs the sleep from his eyes. He pulls some shorts on and inspects the room. It is cluttered but clean. EDDIE is obviously a pack rat – a desk and nightstand are covered in stacks of books and papers, and the bookshelves are crammed to the nines. Curiously enough, there are no posters of Tom Jones, although there is a small but organised collection of CDs and LPs in one corner, easily the tidiest part of the room.

REESE gravitates towards this corner as EDDIE returns.)

REESE: Coast clear?

EDDIE: I think he's still asleep. Sorry, I get up really early…

REESE: No worries. Early bird and all…

(Picking up one of the LPs.)

Tom Jones!

EDDIE: Yeah! It's good, that one!

(Hastily takes it from REESE in order to protect it, then catches himself. If REESE noticed, he doesn't let on.)

One of his first. I'd play it if…

(Glances at the door.)

REESE: He was pretty hot!

EDDIE: Well, yeah!

(Returns the LP to its home.)

REESE: That why you got interested in him?

EDDIE: *(What sacrilege!)* No!

REESE: *(Grins.)* Just asking!

EDDIE: No, I got into him after my mum passed away.

REESE: She like him?

EDDIE: Mum – ? Naw! He'd be a little much for her… Shameful! Too much feeling. Made her uncomfortable. Dad, too.

REESE: Must've been hard for you, growing up.

EDDIE: You mean after she died?

REESE: Both.

(Beat.)

I meant to come 'round afterwards, but…

EDDIE: You didn't know her.

REESE: I knew *you*.

(Beat.)

EDDIE: *(Re: Tom Jones.)* You know, when he was first on the radio everyone assumed he was black…

REESE: Funny, when you first started singing I assumed you were Welsh.

(Pokes him playfully.

Slight beat. EDDIE tries to kiss him, but REESE turns his head.

Grimacing but not unkind.)

You need to brush your teeth…

EDDIE: *(Tentative.)* I'm sorry, I'm kind of new to this –

REESE: *(Taking his hand and pulling him into an affectionate embrace.)* No, I mean you really need to brush your teeth!

(Beat.)

You're doing fine.

(EDDIE looks at him curiously.)

Well, it's obvious you're not a virgin!

(EDDIE grins. Beat.)

EDDIE: Reese… I –

(REESE's mobile rings. He silences it. EDDIE panics, rushing to the door once more. He opens it, peeks his head out as REESE checks his caller ID.

REESE freezes and lights dim everywhere but around EDDIE as he pokes his head back in.)

(To the audience.) Saved by the ringtone! I was about to make a right fool of myself. First off, it's not about the sex – I happen to like women… but I'm open-minded. It's just that Reese and me, we're less like Tom Jones and the missus and more like Tom Jones and – well, Elvis.

(Over the following, 'STAGEHANDS' will present EDDIE with a guitar and bring him forward to an isolated pool of light to begin his song.)

The two met in 1965 on the set of *Paradise Hawaiian Style*. Tom didn't expect him to know who he was… then all of a sudden there he is, arms outstretched and singing Tom's hit song, 'With These Hands'! To the end of the King's days they served as the other's conscience, confidant, inspiration and Father Confessor. Priscilla herself said Elvis was never happier than on those legendary Vegas nights when they would come together after their evening shows, share a childhood story or two, and make beautiful music until the wee hours of the morning. Tom and Elvis: we're like that… except with hot sex.

#11   **Eddie Woo/Come With**   (Eddie, Reese)

Eddie Woo,
Who you gonna tell your troubles to,
Have a laugh with when you're feeling blue
And you can't go on?
Ain't this life a mess,
All alone with just your loneliness,
Spinnin' lies that matter less and less,
'Til the last great con,
When Eddie Woo is gone…?

(REESE steps into an adjacent pool of light with another guitar and sings.)

REESE: Oh, come with, oh, come with,
Eddie Woo, come with,
Oh, come with, oh come with,
Eddie Woo, come with.
I'll come through, Eddie Woo.
Eddie Woo, come with –
I need you so…
Didn't you know?

EDDIE: Eddie Woo,
Do you think about the things you do?
Is there any part that's really you
In that stone cold heart?
Is there love to spare
In this sorry game of truth or dare?
Can you love when you're just empty air,
When you're much too smart?
Oh, what a work of art…

REESE: Oh, come with, oh, come with,
Eddie Woo, come with,
Oh, come with, oh come with,
Eddie Woo, come with.
If you knew, Eddie Woo.
Eddie Woo, come with –
We'll take it slow…
Eddie, let go…

EDDIE: *(Overlapping.)*
'Oh, come with, oh, come with,
Eddie Woo, come with…'

EDDIE, REESE: Oh, come with, oh come with,
Eddie Woo, come with,

Me and you, Eddie Woo,
Eddie Woo, come with –
I want you so…

(Lights fade on EDDIE.)

REESE: Didn't you know?

(The 'STAGEHANDS' remove REESE's guitar as the number ends. The lights come back up on EDDIE and REESE as we left them before EDDIE'S reverie.)

EDDIE: *(Having peeked into the other room.)* He's still asleep!

REESE: Thank God!

EDDIE: Who was that?

REESE: Oh… no one!

EDDIE: You can call them back, just try to keep it down.

REESE: Forget it, it's alright.

EDDIE: *(Trying to be helpful.)* It's six-thirty in the morning, it might have been important…

REESE: Right – let it rest, eh?

EDDIE: *(Taken aback.)* Why won't you tell me?

REESE: We're not getting married!

EDDIE: Good, 'cos I'm not asking! Is it your girlfriend?

REESE: I'm going.

(Dressing.)

EDDIE: Is it your boyfriend?

(REESE ignores him.)

Is it Dillon?

(REESE shoots him a look.)

Oh my God, it's Dillon, isn't it?

REESE: You're a prick.

EDDIE: Get out!

REESE: *(Cooling down.)* Eddie…

EDDIE: Get out!

(REESE grabs his rucksack and exits.

#12   **Baby, We Can Lie All Night**   (Eddie, Sheila, Angela, Dillon)

Music begins as lights change and the set breaks apart. It is as if EDDIE's head has cracked open.

EDDIE performs a sexually-charged, almost angry Tom Jones-style number with SHEILA, ANGELA and DILLON.)

Baby, we can lie all night.
Baby, we can lie all night.
Tell me 'no' when it's alright.
Feed me any line, I'll bite.
I'll be the man you wish you could have.
You be my shield and I'll be your salve.
Oh, baby, we can lie all night.
Baby, we can lie all night.

SHEILA: Baby, we can use our smarts…

ANGELA: Bare our souls but spare our hearts…

DILLON: Skip through all the boring parts…

SHEILA, ANGELA, DILLON: Fill up all our shopping carts…!
If we believe, and baby we do,
Who is to say some part isn't true?
Oh, baby, we can use our smarts.
Baby, we can play our parts.

EDDIE: Maybe I'm an astronaut
And headed for the moon…
Maybe I'm Sir Lancelot
And Arthur's comin' home soon.
I can be your Mister X, whatever your ideal,
Long as we can pull the plug when things start getting real – !
Alright, alright…
Let me whet your appetite.
Baby, we can lie all –
Baby, we can lie all night…!

EDDIE, SHEILA, ANGELA, DILLON: Baby, say we'll both forgive.
Won't you say we'll both forgive?
Truth is all so relative.
Cross my heart and hope to live!
So what if we ain't quite what we say?

EDDIE: You squint your eyes and I'll look away!
Oh –

EDDIE, SHEILA, ANGELA, DILLON: Let's not be so sensitive!
Baby, say we'll both forgive.

EDDIE: Darling, you can be the Queen
And I'm your biggest fan –
Make you think you're seventeen
And just having your first man –
Baby, I can treat you like a major movie star…
Just as long as you don't tell me who you really are!

(They engage in a red-hot pas de quatre…)

That's right, that's right…

Out of mind is out of sight!
Baby, we can lie all –

SHEILA, ANGELA, DILLON: Baby, we can sigh all –

EDDIE, SHEILA, ANGELA, DILLON: Baby, we can lie all –

(EDDIE takes out a coin, flips it, puts it back into his pocket.

A phone ring. SHEILA steps forward in 'real life'.)

SHEILA: *('On the phone'.)* Eddie!

EDDIE: *('On the phone'.)* Sorry to bother you, darling, but you know that encounter group of yours that meets today? At the library?

SHEILA: *(Waking up.)* Yes?

EDDIE: Where shall I meet you?
(Sung.)
Baby, we can lie all night…!

(Blackout.)

SCENE TWO

(The Stratford Library, the following afternoon. EDDIE enters with a small bouquet of flowers, looking for SHEILA.)

EDDIE: *(To the audience.)* Libraries make me nervous the older I get. Must be the eerie silence of all that knowledge, without a single banner ad.

(SHEILA enters, flustered.)

SHEILA: Eddie! You haven't been waiting long?

EDDIE: No, darling, I'm alright.

SHEILA: Dui bu qi, dui bu qi! I was supposed to get my break fifteen minutes ago, but 'Mama Jamaica' over there –
(Over her shoulder.)
– seems to be living on 'black time'!

SHEILA'S CO-WORKER: *(Offstage, in a Jamaican accent.)* Oi, Miss T'ing! This here a library, not a singles bar!

SHEILA: *(To EDDIE.)* Uch! Just ignore her.
(Seeing the flowers.)
For me…?
(Taking them, giddy.)
So… this where I work! I'm sorry to hear about your father, the King; but I'm glad you're here. I've told my friends so much about you!
(Guiding him to the meeting room.)

EDDIE: Well, you know, I think it was our master Confucius who once said, 'One ounce of health is worth ten thousand of gold.'

SHEILA: *(Moaning, pulling him close; sensual.)* Say that again, in Chinese…!

SHEILA'S CO-WORKER: *(Offstage.)* Wha' happen, Brother not good enough for you, girl?

(SHEILA scowls at her.)

SHEILA: *(For the CO-WORKER's benefit.)* Just because *some* of us are interested in *bettering* ourselves!

(To EDDIE, at the meeting room door.)

Now, I just want to warn you, the woman in charge can come on a little strong.

EDDIE: Oh, I like strong women…

SHEILA: Oh! Wear this…

(Reaches into her bag and produces two yellow-coloured half-masks with absurdly long and narrow eye-slits. She hands one to EDDIE.

Putting hers on.)

In here, we're all equals!

EDDIE: *(Amused.)* Right!

(Dons his mask.

And we are in the meeting room of the library. The walls are a bizarre amalgam of Maoist propaganda, one-sheets for various East Asian-centric movies ['Joy Luck Club', 'Dim Sum: A Little Bit of Heart', 'Dragon: The Bruce Lee Story'…] and posters for events such as the 'Concert for British East Asian Awareness' and 'Rally to Take Back the Teahouse'. A rather large hand-drawn poster is the newest addition. It reads 'Rally for the Victims of the 2004 Morecambe Bay Cockling Disaster'.

Around a table strewn with art supplies stand the two other members of SHEILA's 'Racial Encounter Group': a man – masked – who shall go by the name of ELDER BROTHER and, to EDDIE's horror, ANGELA.

EDDIE slowly turns to the audience as if to say, 'Ever have one of those weeks?')

SHEILA: Sorry I'm late! I brought a friend…

ANGELA: Welcome, Brother! Yellow Power!

SHEILA, ELDER BROTHER: *(Raising their fists in the air.)* Yellow Power!

SHEILA: Everyone, this is –

EDDIE: *(Disguising his voice.)* Edmond!

(ANGELA looks at him, curiously.)

SHEILA: *(A little taken aback, but being careful to use the same name.)* Ed*mond*'s my boyfriend. The one I told you about…?

ELDER BROTHER, ANGELA: *(Softening momentarily, variously.)* Oh! Hello! Pleased to finally meet you! etc.

ANGELA: *(Grand.)* Edmond, I want you to meet the charter members of my British East Asian Empowerment Group, the 'Gang of Three'! Elder Brother…

ELDER BROTHER: Yellow Power!

EDDIE: Hello…

ANGELA: … Little Sister…

SHEILA: Yellow Power!

EDDIE: Yes…

ANGELA: *(Indicating herself.)* And Mother Tongue!

EDDIE: *(Feebly.)* Alright…?

ELDER BROTHER: How can we be alright when every day our Yellow Brothers and Sisters are struggling against the tyranny of the Occidental oppressors!

ANGELA: Today, as we honour the Victims of the 2004 Morecambe Bay Cockling Disaster…

(To EDDIE.)

You *are* familiar with the 2004 Morecambe Bay Cockling Disaster?

(Beat; clearly EDDIE has no idea what she is talking about.

ELDER BROTHER: *(Rattling off, impatiently.)* Twenty-one illegal Chinese workers drowned picking cockles in Morecambe Bay in February 2004 because emergency services couldn't understand them when they rang for help!

ANGELA: … we begin with our Affirmations.

(Pulling EDDIE away from SHEILA and into position.)

Here, here, Edmond, stand next to me. Everybody, quick, form a circle!

(They do. All bow their heads in a show of solidarity.

Solemnly, in prayer.)

Dear Great Yellow God… We join together this afternoon with our newest Yellow Brother, Edmond, to give humble thanks for the divine gift of ethnic consciousness and racial self-actualisation. May we bring dignity and honour to all your children, wherever they may be marginalised.

#13   Yellow Power   (Angela, Sheila, Elder Brother, Eddie, Militant Chorus)

(Music starts, pulsing with increasing fervour. As the number progresses, EDDIE becomes more and more disturbed.)

Yellow, my father,
Yellow, my mother,
Yellow, the earth from which I was sprung.
Yellow, my sister,

yellow, my brother,
Yellow, my rice-bowl,
Yellow, my dung!

SHEILA, ELDER BROTHER: Her dung!

ANGELA: My dung!
Yellow Power is yours!
Tell Tom Whitey time to lock all the doors!
Yellow Power, feel it in your drawers…!

SHEILA: Yellow, my honour,
Yellow, my armour,
Yellow, my wardrobe,
Yellow, my nose.

ELDER BROTHER: Yellow, my anger,
Yellow, my hunger,
Yellow, the piss I stream at my foes!

ANGELA, SHEILA: Which piss?

ELDER BROTHER: This piss!

ANGELA: Yellow Power, my friends…
Yellow Power, the crusade never ends!
Tell Ol' Whitey time to make amends!

SHEILA: *(Shouted.)* Green tea!

ELDER BROTHER: *(Shouted.)* Bruce Lee!

ANGELA: *(Shouted.)* Lao Tzu!

EDDIE: *(Shouted, trying to join in.)* Bird flu!

ANGELA: Yellow, my lover,
Yellow, my lager…

SHEILA: Yellow, the locks I yanked in my dreams!
Yellow, my loathing…
Yellow, my longing…
How to describe it?

EDDIE: Yellow, it seems.

SHEILA: Quite right!

ANGELA, ELDER BROTHER: Bright light!
Yellow Power, *en garde*!
Yellow Power –

SHEILA: I was totally scarred!

ANGELA, ELDER BROTHER, SHEILA: Yellow Power –

ELDER BROTHER: Kinda gets me hard…!

EDDIE: *(Moving off.)* Ooh, this is a bit exhausting! I think I'd better sit this next one out –

(ANGELA pulls him to her side dramatically as she takes a dramatic turn. A MILITANT CHORUS appears in EDDIE's imagination and backs her up.)

ANGELA: Yellow's the colour of the rising sun,
Making the palest of the white people run.
Yellow can not burn me,
Wouldn't spurn me,
Will not riddle me with cancerous sores…
Yellow's the tiger in the Asian wood,
Licking his chops where once a white person stood.
Yellow doesn't scare me,
Would beware me,
And well it should…
Mister Caucazh, all of Asia is takin' da 'hood!

(ANGELA, ELDER BROTHER, SHEILA and the MILITANT CHORUS get into 'badass' formation and advance during the following. EDDIE tries to keep up. The moves are not unlike Michael Jackson and his gang members' in the 'Bad' video.)

ANGELA, ELDER BROTHER, SHEILA, MILITANT CHORUS:
Yellow, my mother,
Yellow, my father,
Yellow, my nanny,
Yellow, my dog.
Yellow, our shirttails,
Yellow, our entrails,
Yellow, our toenails,
Yellow, our God…

ANGELA: Whose god?

ELDER BROTHER, SHEILA: Our God!

ANGELA: Yellow Power is nigh…
Tell Ol' Whitey that he need not apply!
Yellow Power is our hue and cry!

ANGELA, ELDER BROTHER, SHEILA, MILITANT CHORUS:
Yellow, my lover,
Yellow, my Brother,
Yellow's the answer,
Yellow is clear.
Yellow is fear.
Yellow is near.
Yellow is here!
Power!

(They freeze for a moment as applause begins, then break, laughing, congratulating each other and nodding like Muppets. The MILITANT CHORUS disappears.

In the hubbub, EDDIE, unthinking, pulls off his mask to wipe his brow.)

ANGELA: Eddie!

EDDIE: *(Feigning surprise.)* Angela!

SHEILA: *(Pulling off her mask and whirling him around to face her.)* 'Angela'?!

EDDIE: Sheila…

ANGELA: *(To SHEILA.)* Oi! Hands off my boyfriend!

SHEILA: *(To EDDIE.)* Are you sleeping with her too?

ANGELA: What do you mean, 'too'?!

(To EDDIE.)

You told me you were in class Friday afternoons!

SHEILA: You told me you were having luncheons with your father, the King!

ELDER BROTHER: *(Aiming it at EDDIE like a weapon.)* Despite being the UK's third-largest immigrant group, the British Chinese have no representation in Parliament!

EDDIE: Look, I can explain –

(To the audience.)

No, no, I really can't.

ANGELA: Are you or are you not in law school?

EDDIE: Well, not –

SHEILA: *(Overlapping.)* Are you or are you not the heir to an island kingdom?

EDDIE: Well, it depends on what you –

ELDER BROTHER: *(Scathing.)* The common cockle is able to jump approximately 5 inches at a time, by extending its leg outside the shell and then contracting it!

EDDIE: What – ?

ANGELA: I gave you my yellow heart…

EDDIE: Darling, listen –

SHEILA: Just like *Joy Luck Club*! Amy Tan was right!

EDDIE: I didn't know how to –

ELDER BROTHER: Yellow Power!

EDDIE: *(To ELDER BROTHER, losing it.)* Will you shut up!

ANGELA: Eddie!

EDDIE: Look, what race are you anyway? Are you even Chinese?

ELDER BROTHER: Could be.

ANGELA: Stop it!

ELDER BROTHER: My surname is 'Lee'.

EDDIE: That don't mean you're Chinese!

SHEILA: *(To EDDIE, near tears.)* God, you're so racist!

ELDER BROTHER: *(Defensive, going quite mad.)* What does a Chinese look like then, eh? Go on, tell me! Does he have slanty eyes? Does he have buck teeth?

(Pulls back the corners of his eyes and gives himself an overbite.)

Is that better? Shall I talk with a Chinese accent? 'I wan-too eat-da roas' pohk…!'

SHEILA: This is really upsetting me…!

ANGELA: *(Suddenly calm, rushing to her defence.)* Eddie, I'm going to have to ask you to leave. You've come into my space and insulted my East Asian friends.

EDDIE: What East Asian friends? She's black and he's probably white!

ELDER BROTHER: You're the only one acting white here.

SHEILA: Oppressors come in all shapes and sizes.

EDDIE: Fine! You want to know what I really do? I work behind the counter. At a Chinese takeaway. At my father's takeaway, if you must know, on Stratford High Street. I'm not in law school. I'm not heir to the throne of some obscure island nation in the China Sea. I've sold no records, won no prizes, have no future prospects, and can't bloody well sing, so tell *that* to your twenty-one illegal Chinese cockles!

ELDER BROTHER: 'Cockle-pickers'!

EDDIE: *I am not gay!*

(Silence as EDDIE surveys the havoc he has wrought. To himself.)

Oh, dear.

(He bolts… beat… then returns to set his mask down on the table before exiting for good.

Beat.)

ELDER BROTHER: *(In awe.)* A takeaway…?

SHEILA: *(Relishing the word.)* A takeaway…!

ANGELA: I can't believe it! A real 'victim of the system'!

(Having a religious experience.)

He must be liberated! Yellow Power!

ELDER BROTHER, SHEILA: Yellow Power!

SCENE THREE

(That night, closing time. The takeaway.

HENRY and EDDIE are closing up. There is an awkward silence between the two, even more than usual. One gets the feeling HENRY would desperately like to connect with his son but does not know how. For his part, EDDIE is preoccupied with the events of the last 24 hours.

Finally:)

HENRY: You know, I still have the book bag from when I was in university, in China. Maybe you can use it.

EDDIE: *(Shrugs.)* Okay.

(Beat; decides to tell the truth.)

Look, about that…

(But HENRY has already retrieved a small messenger bag from behind the counter.)

HENRY: Is the one thing I can take… you know, when I am escaping.

(Hands the bag to EDDIE.)

EDDIE: *(Losing his nerve.)* Thanks…

(EDDIE takes the bag. Silence. He tries another tactic.)

So what time is the photographer coming tomorrow?

HENRY: Afternoon, I am not sure what time. Why?

EDDIE: I was thinking… Big day –

HENRY: Mmm!

EDDIE: Maybe after the picture, we should treat ourselves, take the night off. Kind of as a reward.

HENRY: Why, you have the plans?

EDDIE: Well, no, not anything definite, but…

HENRY: Maybe we take off Monday. Tomorrow is the busiest night!

EDDIE: *(Defeated.)* 'Course.

HENRY: Have to save up for the tuition!

EDDIE: Yeah…

HENRY: For the university –

EDDIE: I know!

(Beat.)

Now that you mention it –

HENRY: I am thinking what do I wear.

EDDIE: Hmm?

HENRY: For the picture. I think maybe the suit is too formal.

EDDIE: Yeah, well…

HENRY: You know, the time change – nowaday, everything more casual…

EDDIE: We're only a takeaway, after all!

HENRY: *(With sudden anger.)* Ey! Do not disrespect your mother like that! She spend all her life building the business, it is her life work! You think, how you are able live, ah? 'Only a takeaway'… Is more than many people have!

(Beat.

Ashamed for having lost his temper, though maintaining 'face'.)

Your idea is wrong, but the feeling is right. A suit – maybe people will think I am trying to show off. Also, make it look like I do no work, like Lum run the entire restaurant and I sit home like the fat cat. Have to have something show the hard work, but not too sloppy, you know.

(Lecturing.)

You have to wear something nice tomorrow, ah?

EDDIE: Don't worry!

HENRY: 'Don't worry'…!

(Closes the shutters. Beat.)

You know, tomorrow we are also going to have the important guest, for the tea. Need to keep that Dillon under control.

EDDIE: Guest?

HENRY: She is the very famous Hong Kong movie star. Widow Chu. You can call her Auntie Chu. She works with many famous people. Cliff Richard, Stevie Wonder…

(He draws a blank.)

You probably do not know her, but she has the unique talent. Sing, act, dancing…

EDDIE: What, did she know Mum?

(Beat.)

HENRY: Why would she know your mother?

EDDIE: Well, where did you meet her? Why haven't you ever mentioned her before?

HENRY: In the teahouse in Chinatown. Very refined, has the big flat in Kensington…

EDDIE: *(Upset.)* Kensington? Wait – have you been there? How long have you been seeing this woman?

HENRY: She is only the friend, okay?

EDDIE: Were you seeing her while Mum was sick?

HENRY: Don't talk like that about your mother!

EDDIE: I'm not, I'm 'talking like that' about you!

HENRY: I am your father!

EDDIE: Yeah, that's what the birth certificate says.

> *(Beat.)*
>
> I'll see you later.
>
> *(Exits.)*

HENRY: *(Calling after him.)* You wear something nice tomorrow!

> *(We follow EDDIE as he storms off into the night. He passes DILLON on her bike on the street coming the other way.)*

DILLON: Eddie!

> *(EDDIE turns around.)*
>
> You close up already? I left my mobile…
>
> *(EDDIE has already taken it out of his pocket and hands it to her.)*
>
> Oh, cheers! Never done that before… I hope you haven't been reading my texts – Wait, on second thought, it's pretty damn good porn.
>
> *(Beat.)*
>
> What's happening tomorrow? You getting off early from work?

EDDIE: Still sorting things out.

DILLON: Well, when you gonna tell him? Your dad… He might surprise you, you know. My parents are over the moon. They're sending him a fruit and cheese basket.

EDDIE: What they have to do that for? You know he hates it. Plus he's lactose intolerant… it's like they're rubbing his nose in it.

DILLON: Well, they appreciate it. You know, your taking care of me.

EDDIE: To him it's flaunting.

> *(Beat.)*

DILLON: You alright?

EDDIE: I just found out Dad has a 'friend'.

DILLON: What, a boyfriend?

EDDIE: *(Disgusted.)* What? Why would you think that?!

DILLON: The way you said it, 'My Dad has a "friend"…'! Like Jeremy Kyle.

EDDIE: 'Widow Chu'. Could you die?

DILLON: He's human, you know. Do you expect him to be alone the rest of his life?

EDDIE: No, just the rest of mine. How would you like it if your dad started shagging another woman?

DILLON: If my mum wasn't around, you mean? More power to him. He's nearly fifty, how many good years does he have left?

EDDIE: Aren't Indians supposed mate for life?

DILLON: I think you're thinking of elephants. Besides, if Mum was gone, that'd settle it, wouldn't it? Contract fulfilled.

EDDIE: That's practical.

DILLON: As Ben Kingsley with a handful of salt.

(Beat.)

Poor thing, you're always expecting the world to make sense. Never has, never will. The sooner you accept that, the sooner you can start focusing on how you make the whole damned mess work for you.

EDDIE: In my next life I want to come back as you.

(Beat.)

DILLON: So what did you do last night?

EDDIE: What…?

DILLON: You and Reese, after I left. Thought maybe if I let you spend some time together on your own, you might – you know, lay off a bit!

EDDIE: *(Vague.)* Oh, yeah… well, you know –

DILLON: Isn't he brilliant?

EDDIE: *(Unenthused.)* He's alright.

(Beat.)

DILLON: *(Annoyed.)* Of course he is…!

EDDIE: Dillon…

DILLON: It's not as if we're getting married, you know! Would it kill you to be happy for me once in a while? You're like a vampire. A joy vampire. 'Oh, look! It's a newborn sparrow! Oh, look! It's a lovely little girl with an ice cream! Oh, look! It's Prince William and Kate Middleton!'

(Makes a horrific sucking sound.)

EDDIE: *(Insistent.)* You can do a lot better!

DILLON: Right, then! Tell me, I want to know: just what sort of living god would meet Eddie Woo's exacting standards?

(EDDIE grabs her and snogs her long and hard.

#14   Come With (Reprise)   (Eddie, Dillon)

They separate.)

Eddie…! I –

EDDIE: Is that alright – ?

DILLON: *(Covering lamely – she has wanted this for a very long time.)* Well, yeah, you know, I mean, you're my best mate –

EDDIE: I love you, you know.

DILLON: *(Overwhelmed.)* Oh, Eddie…

EDDIE: Oh, come with, oh, come with,
Dillon, do, come with.
Yes, it's true, I'll pull through
If it's you I'm with.
Make it new, just we two,
Me and you, come with.
I need you so…
Didn't you know?

DILLON: Is it true, is it true,
Is it you I'm with?
'Cos I knew, yes, I knew,
And I do come with.
Me and you, Eddie Woo,
Yes, its you I'm with.

EDDIE, DILLON: I love you so…

DILLON: About time!

(She pulls him back into another long kiss. Lights fade.)

SCENE FOUR

EDDIE: *(To the audience as he changes into his 'nice clothes'. He holds a television remote.)* There's a clip online you can see of Tom at the start of his career, before he hit big. It's a music show from 1964 called *The Beat Room,* where he sings his first – and unsuccessful – single 'Chills and Fever'. There he stands, onstage in the middle of his first band The Senators, grimacing, gyrating mechanically and flailing his arms like a mad octopus, never once making eye contact with the crowd of well-dressed but unenthused youths executing the latest dance moves for squares. It's a shocking sight… the voice is there, but This Is Most-Certainly-*Not* Tom Jones. Compare it to the clip of his 1965 performance of the same song on Australian telly. The difference couldn't be more striking. Here, Tom stands alone, using his bedroom eyes to devastating effect… his every fist bump and pelvic thrust timed and calculated to elicit the maximum possible scream from his audience of adoring fans. In a year, he has become Tom Jones the international singing sensation: cool, calm and masterfully in control.

(Lights up behind him on the takeaway, Saturday afternoon, tea-time.

A table has been set up with chairs, in the front of the shop – 'squeezed-in' might be a better way to put it. Suffice it to say the takeaway was not designed with table service in mind. One of the enormous widescreen television sets has been mounted above the counter and threatens to devour the entire shop whole.

The 'We'll be back at five o'clock' sign is up in the window.

DILLON enters with her bike. She wears an overcoat despite the warm weather.)

EDDIE: Dillon! *(Checking the clock.)* You're here!

DILLON: *(Very much in love.)* I'm so sorry, darling! Your father sent me home to change into something 'nice'. I don't own anything 'nice'!

EDDIE: It's alright…

(Calming her with a kiss.)

You'll look smashing on telly tonight.

DILLON: You talked to your father!

EDDIE: Not yet, but I've got it all figured out. Look, he's got the hots for this Widow Chu, right? So what we do is butter her up, get her in the mood to celebrate his big day. Convince him to take her out, show her a good time. Maybe even shack up at her place…

DILLON: Serves him right!

EDDIE: Then the only thing we need to worry about is that photographer getting here on time. As soon as he's done, bam, they're out the door and we're off on a train to Central. Got everything I need in here.

(Reveals his father's messenger bag.)

DILLON: Sounds like a plan, just tell me what I can do! Lum's pretty excited. Seems he's a fan. Caught him watching one of her movies on DVD this morning, after they hooked up the widescreen. He was positively catatonic…

EDDIE: Brilliant. We'll use that to our advantage.

(Getting up and setting the remote on his stool.)

By the way, I'm putting the remote on this stool, keep forgetting where I put it last…

(DILLON takes off her overcoat to reveal an over-the-top lehenga choli.)

Whoa!

DILLON: What? It's from my cousin's wedding!

EDDIE: It's a bit much!

DILLON: *(Panicking.)* Well, he said wear something 'nice'! How am I supposed to know what he means?

EDDIE: It's like you wandered in from Taste of bloody Mumbai!

DILLON: Oh my God, oh my God!

(We hear the sound of a car outside. EDDIE rushes to the window.)

EDDIE: Look, just act natural, maybe she won't notice… Remember: make nice!

DILLON: Natural, right… Natural… My bike!

(They look for a place to stash the bike but there is no room, what with the table and chairs. Finally, DILLON opens the utility closet and shoves the bike in, vertically.

The front door opens and in strolls WIDOW CHU, followed by HENRY.)

HENRY: Welcome, welcome!

(WIDOW CHU is clearly taken aback by the meagre surroundings.)

EDDIE: *(With a nod.)* Auntie Chu!

HENRY: This is my son, Edmond.

EDDIE: Did you have a good trip?

WIDOW CHU: Is so far away…! I – ah – get a little carsick…

(She sees DILLON in her lehenga choli and is clearly disoriented.)
Wah…

HENRY: *(Jumping as he sees DILLON for the first time.)* Hwah!

EDDIE: This is my friend Dillon.

DILLON: *(Extending a hand, in a thick Indian accent.)* How do you do?

(EDDIE shoots DILLON a look as WIDOW CHU turns to HENRY for an explanation. While her back is turned, DILLON mouths a frantic apology to EDDIE.)

HENRY: *(Baffled.)* Dillon is our – ah – delivery person!

WIDOW CHU: *(Her gaze returning to DILLON as she imagines her delivering takeaway orders in this outfit.)* Yi?

HENRY: *(Feebly.)* She is… from India.

WIDOW CHU: *(Inscrutable, shaking DILLON's hand uncomfortably.)* Mmm.

HENRY: Dillon, why don't you get us the tea?

DILLON: Yes, sahib.

(To WIDOW CHU.)

You're looking very beautiful, Widow Chu. Isn't she beautiful, Mr. Woo?

(Exits.)

WIDOW CHU: *(To HENRY, sotto voce.)* Is she the lesbian?

HENRY: Edmond! Tell Widow Chu the history of the shop, ah?

EDDIE: Well, my parents opened the shop in 1989, a year before I was born. He decided to call it 'Happy Family' in honour of my birth.

WIDOW CHU: Mmm. I had a son, but he was illegitimate. Then, he died…

EDDIE: Er… We're the first and to-date only Chinese takeaway on High Street. There used to be an Alabama Fried Chicken next door, but it burned down.

WIDOW CHU: … It was in a fire.

(Awkward silence.)

EDDIE: The widescreen telly is a new addition… dating from this morning…

(DILLON enters with a tray of tea.)

HENRY: *(Relieved.)* Ah, here is the tea!

DILLON: *(Serving WIDOW CHU.)* For the beautiful Widow Chu!

(WIDOW CHU shifts away from her, uncomfortably.)

Lum made some special dim sum, for the happy occasion, memsahib!

(LUM enters humbly with a large plate of assorted dim sum and sets it down on the table, afraid to look at WIDOW CHU.)

HENRY: This is our cook, Mr. Lum! He only speaks the Mandarin…

WIDOW CHU: Ah, I only speak the Cantonese.

(To LUM, loudly – as if to a pet.)

Wah! Is the special treat!

(Glances at HENRY.)

Is much better than the chips, ah?

(LUM stiffens.)

LUM: Ah? 'Chips'?

(EXITS quickly.)

HENRY: *(Raising his teacup in a toast.)* This is a rare treat, me and my son and his friend and our honoured guest, Widow Chu! Welcome to our family!

EDDIE: *(A little too enthusiastically.)* Hear, hear!

(HENRY's poor choice of words is not lost on anyone. ALL sip their tea awkwardly.

Beat.)

My father tells me you're a movie star?

HENRY: You will not believe, when she come to town, how many Chinese people camp outside the hotel…

WIDOW CHU: Mmm, yes, but from very long time ago. Probably you will not have heard of my movies.

DILLON: Because they were bad?

WIDOW CHU: Because they are Hong Kong movies.

DILLON: I have seen some Hong Kong movies. Have you worked with John Woo?

WIDOW CHU: No.

DILLON: Jackie Chan?

WIDOW CHU: No.

DILLON: Jet Li?

WIDOW CHU: No.

DILLON: Stephen Chow?

WIDOW CHU: This tea is very fragrant.

HENRY: She is known for acting in other languages.

DILLON: Other than English?

WIDOW CHU: *(Losing her patience.)* Other than the Cantonese...!

HENRY: *(Trying to salvage the situation.)* Ah, how do you do it, Widow Chu?

WIDOW CHU: Every language has the different quality, you know, different history... When I am singing in Russian, the sound is very forceful. I am like the bear. In Latin, I am wise, filled with ancient wisdom. When I am acting in Mexican, I am like fire: hot, fiery... like the flamenco! Each one, is like I become a different person. Is like the whole world in the two lip, ah?

#15   When I Sing   (Widow Chu)

When I sing in French,
You would not believe:
Everybody wiping the tear with their sleeve.
When I sing in French,
Though I am Chinese,
All you think is passion and romance and cheese.
When I sing in Dutch,
It is very loud.
Is because I know that those Dutches are proud...
When it is in Greek,
Greek is very fun...
And you throw the dish on the floor when you're done!
When I sing in Italian, is sexy and wild,
But respecting the God above.
You will think: if Sinatra and me have a child,
She can sing. She can pray. She can love.
When I sing in Thai,
I am like the tease.
Is because the Thai, all they want is to please.
When I sing in Swiss,
I am so aloof...
You are always wanting to show me the proof.
When I sing in Czech,
I am very cold:
You will feel I only will do what I'm told.

While in Lebanese,
It is so profound.
It is like the desert when I make the sound.
There are so many language demand to be sung,
So I sing them with all the heart.
You do not need to travel, just follow my tongue:
Is a trip. Is the gift. Is the art.
For the smart.
When I sing Chinese,
I am nothing new…
So I sing in Russian, Croatian and Mexican, too
And I show you France
And I show you Greece
And the 'global village', I watch it increase…
It is like I'm doing the part for world peace.

DILLON: Brava, Widow Chu! That was beautiful!

(Serving WIDOW CHU some dim sum.)

Have some oysters. I hear they're an aphrodisiac…!

(WIDOW CHU drops her teacup in shock, spilling tea all over the table and floor.)

HENRY: Aiya! Dillon!

DILLON: *(Cleaning up.)* Right away, sahib!

HENRY: Where is the mop…

(Goes to the utility closet and opens it. DILLON's bike tumbles out and falls on top of him, soiling his shirt.)

Aiya!

DILLON: *(Dropping the accent.)* Sorry, sorry!

HENRY: My shirt! The photographer – !

(To DILLON, furious.)

Dillon!

DILLON: Sorry, sorry!

(Half-heartedly maintaining the accent for consistency.)

Come in the back, sahib, I will wash it for you…

(To EDDIE, without accent.)

Oh God, Sorry…!

HENRY: *(To WIDOW CHU.)* Excuse me for a moment…!

(DILLON and HENRY exit, leaving EDDIE and WIDOW CHU.

Beat.)

WIDOW CHU: You resent me.

EDDIE: Beg your pardon?

WIDOW CHU: You do not want me here.

EDDIE: No, no, it's like my father said, 'Welcome to the family'…

WIDOW CHU: I am an actor, you think I cannot tell?

(Beat.)

I do not want to replace your mother.

EDDIE: Well, I can't help feeling you are. I'm sorry.

WIDOW CHU: This, too, I know.

EDDIE: And what about your Mr. Chu? Aren't you supposed to honour his memory? That's what my mum said. 'Never divorce, never remarry'.

WIDOW CHU: Edmond… There is something your generation never understand about the older generation. You always say you are trapped between two world: the western, and the traditional. You think your friend is the western and your parent is the traditional. Never think: we are over here, too. Also trapped between the two world. Your father and me, we are brought up with one set of values, but here, everything is changed. Worse than you, we cannot even speak the language well. Barely understand each other. Barely can read the package in the supermarket. Is not just lonely in the heart. Is lonely in the being.

(Beat.)

Besides, when the love is true, like your father for your mother, or me for my husband, Mr. Chu, before he died… no one can replace. Is like my night with Tom Jones.

EDDIE: Tom Jones!

WIDOW CHU: He is probably too old, you do not know him.

EDDIE: Of course I know Tom Jones!

WIDOW CHU: Well, he and I have the – you know – the dalliance.

EDDIE: No!

WIDOW CHU: Mmm! When I am in Las Vegas, appearing at the Sands Hotel. You know the Sands Hotel?

EDDIE: Sure.

WIDOW CHU: He is at the Caesar's Palace. Invite me to come watch him perform… Wah, so sexy. So hairy. Afterward, we have the night of passion in his suite. Such a view of the Strip, you would not believe… Then, in the middle of the lovemaking, he call out a name. But is not my name. Is the name of his wife.

EDDIE: Linda.

WIDOW CHU: Mmm. I hear sometimes he have more than two hundred mistress in a year, and in the middle of lovemaking, he confuse me, a Hong Kong movie star, with his wife. I think, 'This is the true love I can never replace.' And back then, I am very beautiful and skilled in the bedroom… So you see, your mother? You do not have to worry.

(Beat.)

EDDIE: You slept with Tom Jones?

WIDOW CHU: *(Correcting him with a smile.)* Tom Jones sleep with *me*!

(Suddenly, we hear VOICES from outside.)

VOICES: *(Offstage, continuing under.)* Free Eddie Woo! Free Eddie Woo!

(EDDIE looks out the window.)

EDDIE: Oh, no…

(Bolts out of the door.

DILLON and HENRY enter.)

HENRY: What is that sound?

(Looking outside.)

Ah?!

(To DILLON.)

Ey, Dillon, go see what my son is doing…

WIDOW CHU: Mmm…

(Suddenly, the door opens and ANGELA, SHEILA and ELDER BROTHER enter with EDDIE hot on their tail.)

ANGELA, SHEILA, ELDER BROTHER: Free Eddie Woo! Free Eddie Woo! Free Eddie Woo! Free Eddie Woo!

HENRY: *(Overlapping.)* Ey ey ey – ! We are closed!

EDDIE: Come on, please, out, out!

HENRY: 'Free Eddie Woo'! Free him from what?!

ANGELA: Oppression, my father, oppression! We demand Eddie Woo be released from the shackles of family servitude and be free to pursue his dreams!

ELDER BROTHER: Imperialist!

SHEILA: Colonialist!

ANGELA, SHEILA, ELDER BROTHER: Yellow Power!

ELDER BROTHER: For too long, the older generation has mortgaged away the dreams of its children!

SHEILA: For far too long, the younger generation has been poisoned by the humiliations of the past!

ANGELA: For far too long, the Dragon has been imprisoned by the machinations of his fathers –

HENRY: Get out of my shop!

DILLON: Who are these people?

ANGELA: We are the 'Gang of Three'!

ELDER BROTHER: *(Indicating himself.)* Elder Brother…

SHEILA: *(Indicating herself.)* Little Sister…

ANGELA: *(Indicating herself.)* And Mother Tongue! Empowerment *for* Asians –

ANGELA, SHEILA, ELDER BROTHER: *By* Asians!

ANGELA: *(To DILLON.)* Incidentally, when we say Asian, we *don't* mean you…

(DILLON, HENRY and WIDOW CHU are stunned into silence

Stilted, reading from a handwritten sheet.)

'Dear Eddie, we forgive you for the pain you have caused us and want you to know we understand… understand that the lies you have told are but a cry of help from an oppressed heart. Help us to help you to throw off the yoke of oppression so you may return to our loving circle a renewed man. Yellow Power!'

EDDIE: Guys, guys, I'm fine without the help, really!

SHEILA: *(Even more stilted, reading from another handwritten sheet.)* 'Dear Eddie, do not hate us. All we feel for you is love and forgiveness. Please understand you do not have to be a lawyer or foreign prince. You in your divine yellowness are enough. Please be grateful for our intervention, that you may return to our hearts and beds – '

HENRY: Ah?!?!

(Beat as jaws drop all around. EDDIE would crawl into a hole if he could.)

DILLON: Whoa…!

ANGELA: *(To ELDER BROTHER.)* Get the straps…!

(ELDER BROTHER exits.)

DILLON: *(Pushing EDDIE.)* 'Our hearts and beds'?!!

ANGELA: *(Pushing DILLON off of EDDIE.)* Oi! Hands off my boyfriend!

SHEILA: *(To ANGELA.)* What do you mean your boyfriend?!

HENRY: *(To EDDIE.)* I cannot believe – my son with the – with the –

SHEILA: *(To HENRY, pointed.)*
What, 'librarian'?!

(All hell breaks loose. The following lines are spoken simultaneously.)

HENRY: *(To SHEILA.)* Is always the same with you people! Rob the store, call in the phony order, always think about the sex! Say the 'eff this' and the 'eff that', everything is the 'effing', then you wonder why is it you have the teen pregnancy! You want to do it to your own people, fine! Why you have to mess around with the Chinese as well?

SHEILA: *(To HENRY.)* Who's the liar here, eh? Who's the cheat? I've seen *Joy Luck Club*, I know how Chinese men can be. But I thought, 'No, Eddie's different, he's a Prince! How many Chinese men you know who are Princes?' Well, turns out 'none'! Amy Tan, you tell it like it is! Like father, like son, you bloody racist!

ANGELA: *(To DILLON, advancing on her and forcing her back behind the counter.)* You tart! I gave him my yellow heart! We drank from the cup of social injustice and made pools of beautiful yellow pride! Took the language of racial oppression and turned it into our secret language of love! We could have had something special, like Romeo and Juliet, except everyone lives, and played by Chinese people!

DILLON: *(To ANGELA, retreating as she is forced behind the counter.)* Whoa! Back off, Lucy Liu! You know what? You're welcome to him. I'm over it, all of it: Chinese widows, Chinese food, crazy Chinese bitches. You think you're all so smart, but you know what you are? Selfish bastards, the whole lot of you. 'Yellow Power', my ass. More like 'Yellow Shower'!

(DILLON inadvertently sits on the remote. The television set comes on, at full volume. All gasp and cover their ears. WIDOW CHU looks up and is shocked to see her own gigantic, tear-stained face appear on the screen, to deafening music. It is one of her films, playing on DVD. The one in 'Mexican'…)

WIDOW CHU: Hah?!

WIDOW CHU'S VOICE: *(From the television set, in bad Spanish.)* Pero no comprendes, Alejandro, mi amor: te amo! Te amo como nadie ha amado nunca!

(LUM runs out of the kitchen with a metal bucket and stands proudly before WIDOW CHU.)

LUM: 'Chips'!

(He dumps a bucketful of sizzling chips on her plate. WIDOW CHU screams.

The front door opens and REESE enters with a bouquet of flowers.)

REESE: Hullo…?

(Blackout.)

SCENE FIVE

(Immediately following, outside the takeaway.

A PHOTOGRAPHER stands near the entrance, fiddling with her camera.

REESE storms out, followed by EDDIE , messenger bag in hand.)

REESE: *(Throwing the flowers at EDDIE.)* Get off! I feel dirty, which is a lot for *me* to say!

EDDIE: You've got some nerve! At least I was single!

REESE: By thirty-six hours!

EDDIE: So now we're even!

(REESE throws up his hands.)

Besides, wasn't it you who said we were just messing about? 'It's not like we're getting married'! What was I to think?

REESE: Oh, no, that's not how this works! You used me!

EDDIE: And what were you doing to poor Dillon?

(Notices the PHOTOGRAPHER for the first time, smiles and nods. Then, continuing, to REESE.)

All that flirting and talk about her bloody dreams!

REESE: *(Blathering.)* Wha – I –

(Completely irrational.)

It's what I do!

EDDIE: That's not fair.

REESE: *(Stammering. This is a big moment for him.)* Look, I thought –

EDDIE: What – ?

(HENRY and DILLON come barrelling out of the shop, DILLON with her bike.)

HENRY: *(To REESE.)* You! You don't come around here any more, corrupt my son… encourage him to do the singing, have the black girlfriend!

(And the moment has passed.)

REESE: He doesn't need any help from me, Mr. Woo.

(To EDDIE.)

I'm out.

(Exits.

EDDIE looks to DILLON.)

DILLON: *(To EDDIE.)* You could have told me the truth. I could've handled it. Or did you want to have a good laugh?

EDDIE: Dill – You're the one, you've got to see that…

DILLON: You're disgusting. Both of you.

(Gets on her bike.)

HENRY: *(To DILLON.)* Where are you going? You go inside, clean up!

DILLON: So sack me, you old fart.

(Exits, riding off.

Beat.)

HENRY: *(To EDDIE.)* What is she talking about? I don't understand.

(EDDIE gives his father a look.)

Okay, okay, you go back inside, calm your girlfriends, straighten up. Make sure your Auntie Chu is okay.

EDDIE: No. I'm going to that competition.

HENRY: Ah?! You have the nerve?! You ruin my big day, you lie about the A-level, you sleep with the black girl, you humiliate me in front of your friend, in front of Lum, in front of your Auntie Chu, and now you say you want to go on the telly and be the embarrassment, humiliate me in front of the whole world? You cannot sing! If you are so talented, why are you the assistant manager of your father's takeaway, you ask yourself that! Even if you have the talent, you think the white people want to vote for you? Are you really that stupid? You are Chinese! They are not going to want the oriental for the pop star! Huh. Think you are the next Bruce Lee. People are going to laugh at you! You want to go, you don't come back home afterward, I am done with you! Do you hear me?

(Silently, EDDIE removes his keys from his pocket and hands them to his father. HENRY snatches them from him.)

Your mother would be ashamed.

EDDIE: Yeah. Good thing she's not around anymore.

(HENRY is stunned.

EDDIE exits.

HENRY watches him leave, then turns to go back in, noticing the PHOTOGRAPHER for the first time.)

HENRY: Aw, hi, hi. You – ah – want to come in for a drink?

PHOTOGRAPHER: No, no, I'm good.

HENRY: *(Confused.)* Aw…

PHOTOGRAPHER: *(Re: EDDIE.)* Kids, huh?

HENRY: Yes, yes… He – he is a good boy, really… he just get into his mood.

PHOTOGRAPHER: Mmm hmm.

(Beat.)

HENRY: He will be back, I know. Maybe can you come back later, get us both in the shot? Would be a very nice picture…

PHOTOGRAPHER: Oh, no, that's alright. I've gotten the shots I need, actually.

HENRY: Ah? Okay – what about the interview?

PHOTOGRAPHER: Well, honestly, there's not really going to be much room for anything more than a line or two. It's for our 'Fifty Local Eats for under Five Pounds' column. Do you know it?

HENRY: *(Crestfallen.)* Aw. Yes, yes, of course.

PHOTOGRAPHER: I will take a menu, though.

HENRY: *(Avoiding his gaze.)* Oh, okay. Wait here, I get one for you.

(Goes in.)

SCENE SIX

(Stratford Station.

EDDIE enters a train carriage, waiting for the next departure for Central London. He has the release form in hand. By now it is quite tattered.)

As he enters the carriage, the messenger bag gets caught between the doors. EDDIE pulls and pulls and lands in a heap in the middle of the car. A PASSENGER and her FRIEND, sitting opposite him with their backs to the audience, snigger to themselves.)

EDDIE: *(Railing at the PASSENGER and her FRIEND, finally losing it.)* What?! What?! I'm right bloody here, you know! I'm not a bloody leprechaun, I'm not bloody invisible!

(The PASSENGER and her FRIEND get up and move to another carriage.)

Yes, right! You'd better run! Run or the big bad Chinese fella gonna rough you up!

(By this time, the PASSENGER and her FRIEND have gone. EDDIE, alone, continues to rail at them like a lunatic as he tries to repair the strap on the messenger bag, which has been torn.)

You won't be laughing so hard when I win that competition tonight! Maybe you can drool over my picture at the takeaway, if I bother sending one to the local paper! In any case, it's the closest you or my father will ever get to me 'cos whatever happens, I'm never coming back this way again. Snap!

(The messenger bag is a lost cause. This is the final straw for EDDIE, who sits in the middle of the carriage like a child, desperately trying to fix the strap.)

Oh, God…

(Suddenly, the carriage doors open and in walks TOM JONES, circa 1980. He is in his trademark tight leather pants and open shirt, with a full head of curly black hair and a gold cross around his neck.)

#16   A Divine Intervention   (Guardian Angel – Tom Jones)

TOM JONES: Shwmae, Eddie?

(EDDIE leaps to his feet and looks to the PASSENGERS in the other carriages and on the platform.)

They can't see me, Eddie. Only True Disciples can.

EDDIE: What – how – ?

TOM JONES: I come to my flock in times of need. And you, my dear
Chinese boy, are in grave need…
(Sung.)
You got sump'm on your fevered mind?
You got yourself into a nasty bind?
You lookin' for a little counterplan?
Well, you in luck 'cos I'm a macho man!
Whoa whoa whoa whoa –

(Spoken.)

That's right!

(Sung.)

You need a little Tom Jones!
You need a little Tom Jones!
I'm swank,
I'm frank,
Got a great big shank,
When I swing it, how the people shout!
I'm gold,
I'm bold
And a wee bit old,
But I'm here to sort you out!
Now let me get this in a thought or less:
(Closes his eyes and puts his fingers to his temples, utilising his Tom Jones ESP.)

You lost your mama and your life's a mess!

EDDIE: That's right!

TOM JONES: Well, let me summon up my 'sex-o-phones',
Shake my body like I got no bones!
Whoa whoa whoa whoa –

(Spoken.)

Hold tight!

(Sung.)

You got a little Tom Jones!
You got a little Tom Jones!

(He dances. EDDIE is swept along, joining him.)

I'm chic,
I'm cheek,
Got a man's physique,
Show me trouble and I up and pounce!

I'm sleek,
I'm freak
And a bit antique,
But I've got it where it counts!
Now, listen, I don't condescend,
So let me listen to my Chinese friend!
You got a problem like a atom bomb?
Well, lay it on your little Uncle Tom!
Whoa whoa whoa whoa –

(Spoken.)

That's right!

(Sung.)

Whoa whoa whoa whoa –

(Spoken.)

Hold tight!

(Sung.)

Whoa whoa whoa whoa –

(Spoken.)

I'm a knight!

(Sung.)

And a little Tom Jones!
I'm a little Tom Jones!
Have a little Tom Jones!

EDDIE: I'm gonna show 'em, Mr. Jones! I'm gonna get up there and use every trick you ever taught me. Every pelvic thrust, every boot-shaking yelp... That come-hither stare that says 'Strip me down and worship me like the insatiable Sex God you need me to be!' And when I'm through, they're not going to be thinking, 'Wow, that bloke's something else, for a Chinese guy'... They'll be wishing... aching... *praying* they could be Chinese, too...

TOM JONES: Whoa there, Eddie, slow down... you're boiling like pea soup! If you think this talent competition is going to be the answer to all of your problems, well... it's all the dream of a witch according to her will.

EDDIE: I can do it, Mr. Jones. I've got it in me. I just wish –

TOM JONES: What, Eddie?

EDDIE: Well, you must have had a secret. Something to keep you going when times were rough. When you were stuck in that bed with TB, trapped in that glove factory as an apprentice glove cutter... when you knew you had to get away.

TOM JONES: Ah, but you've missed the point entirely, lad. I was never trying to get away. All the sexual bombast, the vocal pyrotechnics, the fancy footwork – that's not what makes Tom Jones Tom Jones. Well, it is, but what I mean is, none of that's going to make a lick of difference if you're running away from who you are. It doesn't count unless it comes from… in here.

(Pats his bare chest.)

This open shirt, these tight leather pants, this gold cross around my neck, this Welshman's afro – they come from a childhood in Pontypridd, nicking records from the corner shop with my fellow Teddy Boys, listening to Chuck Berry and Jerry Lee Lewis on Record Roundup and gospeling up the hymns in church every Sunday.

(Beat.)

I forgot that once, when my good friend and manager Gordon Mills convinced me I should start recording country music. And the results were far from pretty.

EDDIE: I liked 'The Country Side of Tom Jones'…

TOM JONES: Then you're a damned fool. The point is, things never worked out for old Tom Jones, 'less I embraced my roots. I didn't run from 'em. They're a part of my song, and it makes it that much sweeter each time I come on home.

(Beat.)

And what's your song, my yellow friend? What goes into making an Eddie Woo?

(A moment as EDDIE ponders how to answer this.)

EDDIE: I can't –

TOM JONES: Sure, you can. Just listen.

(Pats his bare chest.)

From here.

(EDDIE looks around himself, then at his bag.)

#17   What Makes an Eddie Woo?   (Eddie)

EDDIE: *(Searching.)*
A broken strap.
A swollen arm.
A cheery 'That's alright', 'cos really, what's the harm?
The way you're always finding something dragging from your shoe…
What makes an Eddie Woo?

TOM JONES: Good.

(EDDIE gives him a questioning look.)

Go on.

EDDIE: *(Looking at himself.)*
A tatty shirt.

A sweaty brow.
The kind of glasses they should really not allow.
A grimy bedroom window with a tiny alley view…
What makes an Eddie Woo?
What makes him cool.
What makes him hot.
What does he brings
What has he got.
Where does he fit?
And is he fun?
What makes him tick?
What makes him run?
An achy head.
A racing clock.
A lot of simple questions and a total block.
The growing confirmation that you haven't got a clue – !
What can an Eddie do?
What makes an Eddie Woo?

TOM JONES: *(Gently.)* Sounds like you're on your way to a hit record.

(Begins to leave.)

EDDIE: Wait… where are you going?

TOM JONES: My work is done! I've got an album of Romani folk songs to record next. It sounds far-fetched, but I think I may just get it to work.

EDDIE: But what am I supposed to do?

TOM JONES: You'll figure it out: don't forget, you're a Disciple!

(Beat.)

Long live Wales… And beware of the Martians.

(TOM JONES disappears in a puff of testosterone.

Beat. EDDIE continues, deep in thought.)

EDDIE: The clever dodge
That gets you by.
The lie that's been so long you can't remember why.
The constant, wearing panic that if people really knew…
What makes an Eddie Woo?
The heavy snog.
The frantic kiss.
The mornings praying, 'God, let there be more than this.'
The endless secret pining for the things you won't pursue…
What makes an Eddie Woo?
When will you stop?
When do you choose?
When will you find

What's yours to lose?
Or will you sink
And wash ashore
Before you learn
What Eddie's for?
The world just always out of range.
The sudden, certain dawning something has to change.
'Cos what if what's inside you isn't always what is true?
What else is Eddie Woo?
What makes an Eddie Woo?

(Beat. Thoughtful.)

A Mum and Dad
In monochrome.
A faded picture of a place that once was home.
An agonising emptiness that only grew and grew…
Goodbye to Eddie 'Who?'
And all you're going through.
What will you grow into?
What makes an Eddie Woo…?

CONDUCTOR: *(Voiceover.)* Last call for the 4:58pm East London Line train to Liverpool Station. Last call…

(EDDIE is still as the train begins to move.)

SCENE SEVEN

(That evening, the takeaway. It is just starting to get dark outside.

The table has been put away and the dishes stacked. WIDOW CHU is alone onstage, helping to do the final straightening up for the night.

LUM enters from the kitchen and gives a little bow to WIDOW CHU.)

LUM: Chu Tai Tai… Wan an.

WIDOW CHU: Thank you, Lum.

(In bad Mandarin.)

Xie xie, Lum Xian Sheng.

(This makes LUM's day.)

LUM: Lao ban, wan an!

(HENRY emerges from the kitchen, waves half-heartedly to LUM. LUM exits happily.)

WIDOW CHU: It is your busiest night. You are not going to reopen?

HENRY: How can I? I only have the cook.

WIDOW CHU: What more do you need? Cook, boss, waitress…?

(Indicates herself on the last.)

HENRY: I guess I am not in the mood. Can you believe, since 1989, only close three days: the day Edmond is born, the night of his school play, the day of his mother's funeral.

WIDOW CHU: School play!

HENRY: Yes. He play the Admiral Nelson's boot.

WIDOW CHU: Must have been very special performance. Not even close when your wife pass away…

(Beat.)

Tell me, shouldn't it be 'Lin'?

HENRY: Mmm?

WIDOW CHU: That Lum. Why does he go by his Cantonese last name if he can only speak Mandarin?

HENRY: I have never thought to ask.

WIDOW CHU: Mmm. This country does the strange thing to people… I like your son. He has the conviction.

HENRY: *(He has been waiting to talk about this all evening.)* He is usually the very good boy! That Reese. Don't know where they meet… Is the very bad influence. Give him these crazy idea about the contest! Encourage him to find the girlfriend!

WIDOW CHU: *(Knowing.)* I do not think he would encourage your son to find the girlfriend.

HENRY: Ah? How are you so sure?

WIDOW CHU: You will understand some day.

HENRY: *(Perplexed.)* Aw.

WIDOW CHU: But these girlfriend…! That Angela…! Uhy!

(They share a chuckle.)

Never do I think a Chinese will say, 'Thank God for the black girlfriend'!

(They laugh.)

HENRY: The 'Gang of Three'!

(They laugh hysterically.

Beat.)

Thank you very much for – ah –

(Gesturing at the cleanup job WIDOW CHU has done.)

I am very embarrassed…

WIDOW CHU: Aw, is nothing. Is nostalgic. Once I play the part of a cleaning woman. In Afrikaans…

HENRY: I… very much appreciate you are here. Make the day much easier.

WIDOW CHU: *(Awkward.)* Mmm.

HENRY: We make a good team, ah?

    (Beat.)

WIDOW CHU: You are a good friend, Henry. I am thinking this is how it should be for now.

HENRY: Ah…?

WIDOW CHU: You lost your wife. Today you have lost your son. Me, I do not want to be the safety net. Also, today as I am a part of your family, I see something that is not always clear to me:

    (He looks at her, questioning.)

    I like being the single!

    (Beat.)

    You will be alright?

HENRY: *(Nods.)* Mmm.

WIDOW CHU: Mmm! Good…! Go home…

    (A car horn is heard outside. HENRY is startled by it. WIDOW CHU collects her things.)

    I have called a car… I would like to see how your son sings tonight, but I do not think I should watch with you! Thank you for the tea. Call if you must… but not too late, ah?

    (She waves goodbye to him and exits.

    We hear the car door slam. The car speeds off.

    Complete silence.

    HENRY begins to weep uncontrollably. He cries for a few moments, then stops himself.

    He picks up the remote and turns on the television set and flips the channels until he hits a promo for 'Britain's Newest Unexpected Singing Sensation', coming up at 7:30. He watches quietly.

    EDDIE enters without his noticing and watches HENRY for a moment. HENRY is clearly looking at the screen intently, searching for EDDIE.

    Finally, EDDIE shuts the door behind him. HENRY jumps, turning off the set. He turns and sees EDDIE.

    They stare at one another for a moment, then come together in a silent embrace. They hold on to each other tight – if not for the first time, then for the first time in a long while.

    They separate.)

HENRY: *(Saving face.)* I am checking out the HD channel. Think maybe I spend more than I have to on the 1080p, you know?

EDDIE: No, I think you made the right choice. Successful business has to have the top quality!

HENRY: Not so successful…

EDDIE: No…?

(HENRY gives him a look that speaks volumes. EDDIE understands.)

Then we'll make it that way.

HENRY: Mmm. Have conviction. Like father, like son.

(EDDIE smiles.)

You know, Lum has to leave early tonight, I think, 'How can we stay open without a cook!'

(Tossing EDDIE's keys back to him.)

Did you know there is a karaoke bar close by? Maybe you can sing for your old man!

EDDIE: *(Heading behind the counter to start locking up.)* Maybe!

HENRY: I promise I will clap the loudest!

(EDDIE stops and looks at the picture of his mother on the wall.)

EDDIE: Where's the camera…?

(Begins searching for it in the drawers behind the counter.)

HENRY: Aiya, forget it, I do not need it.

EDDIE: No, wait – Get over there…

(He's found it. He gestures HENRY in front of the counter and begins moving back from it, towards the front of the store, trying to balance it on a ledge here, a chair there, unsuccessfully.)

HENRY: Aiya, be careful! Is not worth it to break…

EDDIE: Hold on, I'll get it – !

(EDDIE keeps on backing up, trying to frame the shot well. He opens the front door and stands in the doorway.)

Okay, I just need to get a chair…

(But someone has snatched the camera from EDDIE. It is REESE. A beat as they regard each other, then REESE motions EDDIE next to HENRY.)

REESE: Go.

(EDDIE stands next to HENRY.)

Alright, smile…

(EDDIE puts his arm awkwardly around HENRY.)

One, two, three…!

(As REESE snaps the shot, lights fade as we see a projection of the photo of HENRY and EDDIE, father and son.)

#18   Finale/Curtain Call   (Company)

(The characters re-emerge in a dreamland, whether of EDDIE's or our making, it is unclear. But they emerge in happy pairings which may or may not suggest their futures: HENRY and EDDIE; DILLON and LUM; ANGELA and SHEILA; and REESE and WIDOW CHU. We get the distinct impression they have all begun the long journey of finding themselves. Except for TOM JONES, because he, after all, knows all.)

APPENDIX

THE *TAKEAWAY* GUIDE TO CONVERSATIONAL MANDARIN

Wo bu ming bai. *I don't understand.*

Wo jiu shi bu ming bai! *I just don't understand! (Wilful)*

Wo shi chong Beijing lai de! Sha gua! *I'm from Beijing! Idiot! (Lit.: 'Stupid melon')*

Hai yao ting xiao hai de hua…! Ba ni de na hua er kan diao! *I have to listen to a child…! I'll cut off your thing!*

Ey?! Shei shuo ni ke yi jing lai de! *Huh?! Who said you could come in here!*

Ni shi wo qing ai de ren! *You're my dear one!*

Ni zhe ge xiao qi gui! Qu ni ma de! *You cheapskate! Go to your Mum's! (Vulgar)*

Ni bu yao lian de dongxi! *You faceless thing!*

Wo pei! *I spit! (Suggested: 'On you')*

Aiya, Ma…! Ni bie ku le! *Uch, Mum…! Stop crying, already!*

Wo xiang nian ni zhe me duo, wo xiang zi sha le! *I miss you so much, I'm going to kill myself!*

Dui bu qi, dui bu qi! *Sorry, sorry!*

Shen me? Shen jing bing! *What? Crazy!*

Ni zhe ge ren: you ben, you ben zhuo, you chou! Hen si ni! *You: dumb, clumsy and ugly! I hate you!*

Chu Tai Tai… Wan an. *Mrs. Chu… Goodnight.*

Xie xie, Lum Xian Sheng. *Thank you, Mr. Lum.*

Lao ban, wan an! *Boss, goodnight!*